This book couldn't have been written, designed and published without an incredible effort on the part of so many people.

I want to personally thank our Duffy & Partners team for all their contributions to this book. Our creative director Dan Olson and senior designer Ken Sakurai made the pages come to life visually. My managing partners, Tricia Davidson and Eric Block, helped in countless ways. And Bridget Schumacher, our project manager, kept all of us on track along the way.

The Duffy & Partners team also extends our gratitude to the writer, Russ Stark, for his time and talent. And to The One Club, particularly Mary Warlick and Yash Egami, for their faith, encouragement and hard work in helping this project come to life.

Finally, our thanks to all of the contributors whose work you're about to enjoy. I hope you're as inspired by their efforts as I am.

JOE DUFFY

DESIGN & EDITING

Duffy & Partners
710 2nd Street South, Suite 602
Minneapolis, Minnesota 55401
TEL 612-548-2333
FAX 612-548-2334

Duffy & Partners believes stronger, smarter design multiplies a brand's value in the marketplace. Founded in 1984, Duffy & Partners has established a reputation for using compelling and strategic design to build brands. Duffy's award-winning work spans all design disciplines including corporate identity, brand identity, packaging design, new media, and environmental design. Clients have included, among others: Atlantis Resorts, Coca-Cola, Jim Beam, Kellogg's, McDonald's, Mona Lisa Hotels, St. Paul Travelers, Sony, Starbucks, The Thymes and Toyota. Duffy & Partners is based in Minneapolis. Additional information can be found at www.duffy.com.

PUBLISHER

One Club Publishing
21 East 26th Street
New York, NY 10010
First published in the United States of America in 2005 by One Club Publishing.

COPYRIGHT

© 2005 One Club Publishing

ISBN
0-929837-25-8

Printed in Singapore

BRAND APART

JOE DUFFY

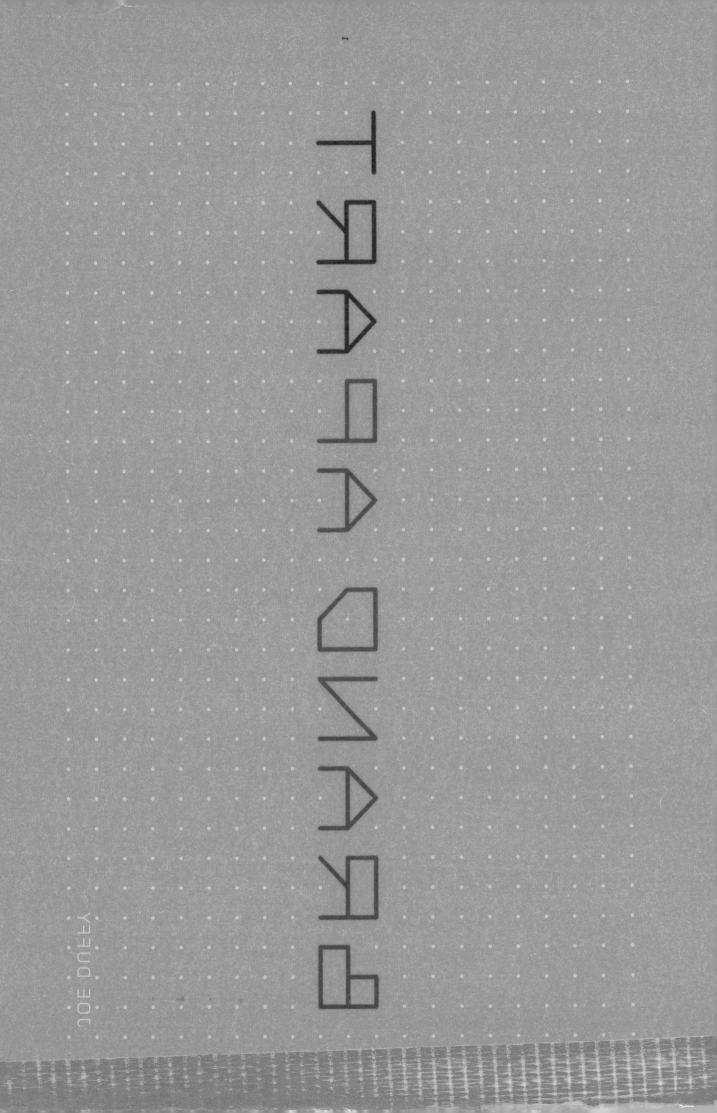

Insights on the art of creating a distinctive brand voice

Insights on the art of creating a distinctive brand voice

CONTENTS

CONTENTS

CONTENTS

4

CONTENTS

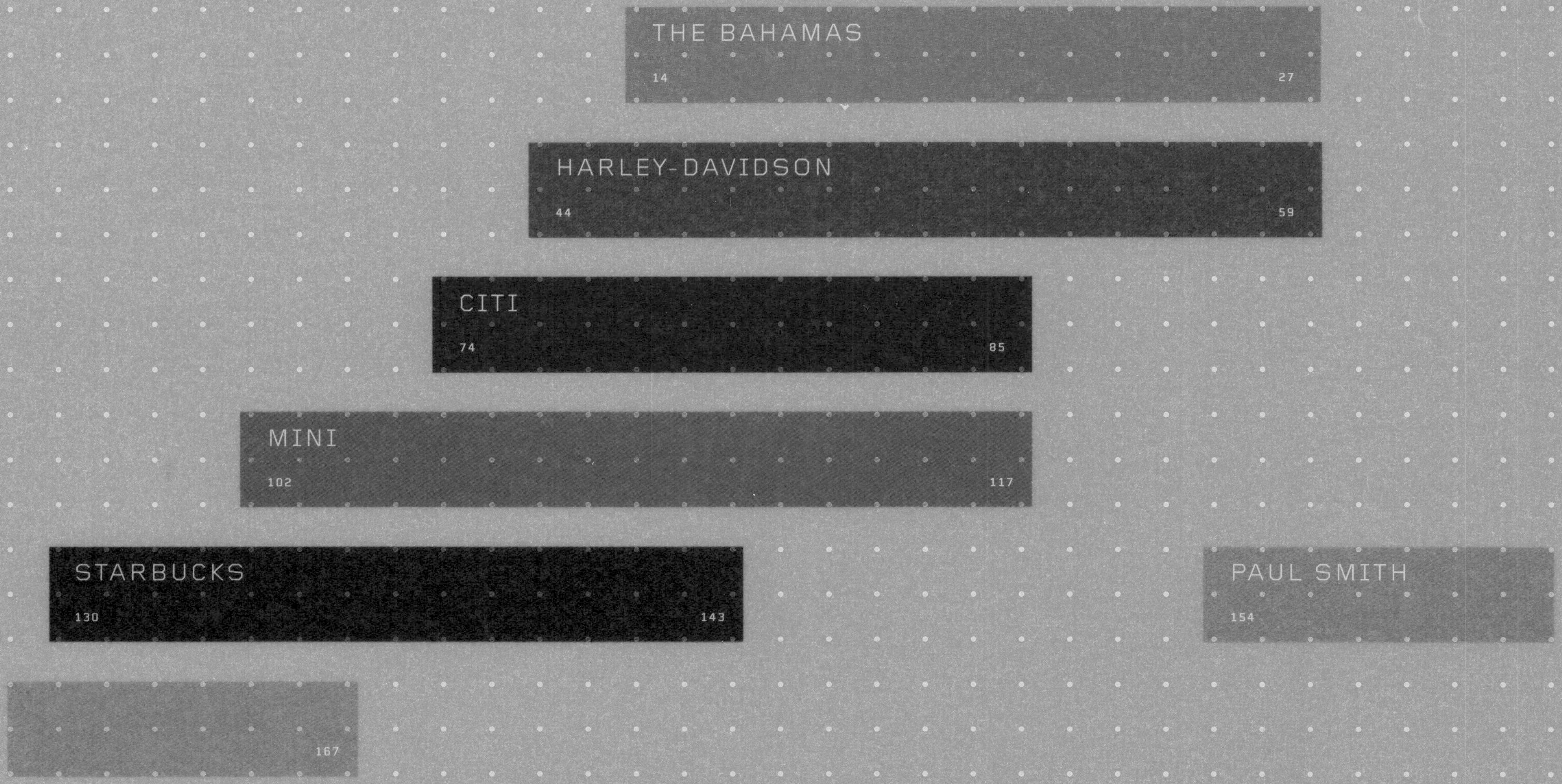

THE BAHAMAS 14 27

HARLEY-DAVIDSON 44 59

CITI 74 85

MINI 102 117

STARBUCKS 130 143

PAUL SMITH 154 5

167

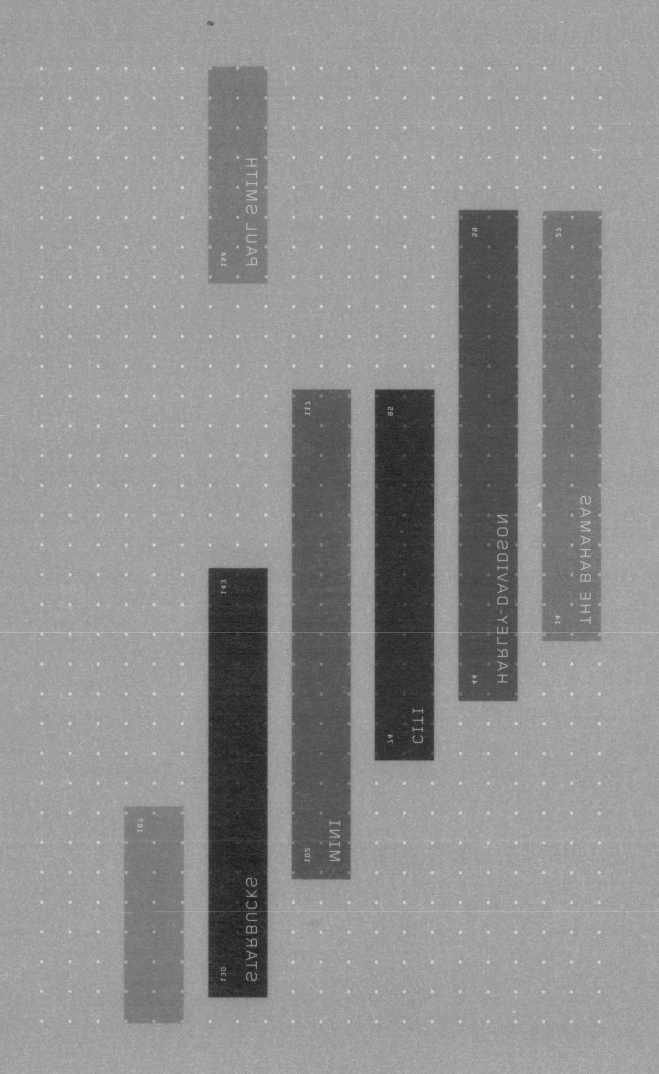

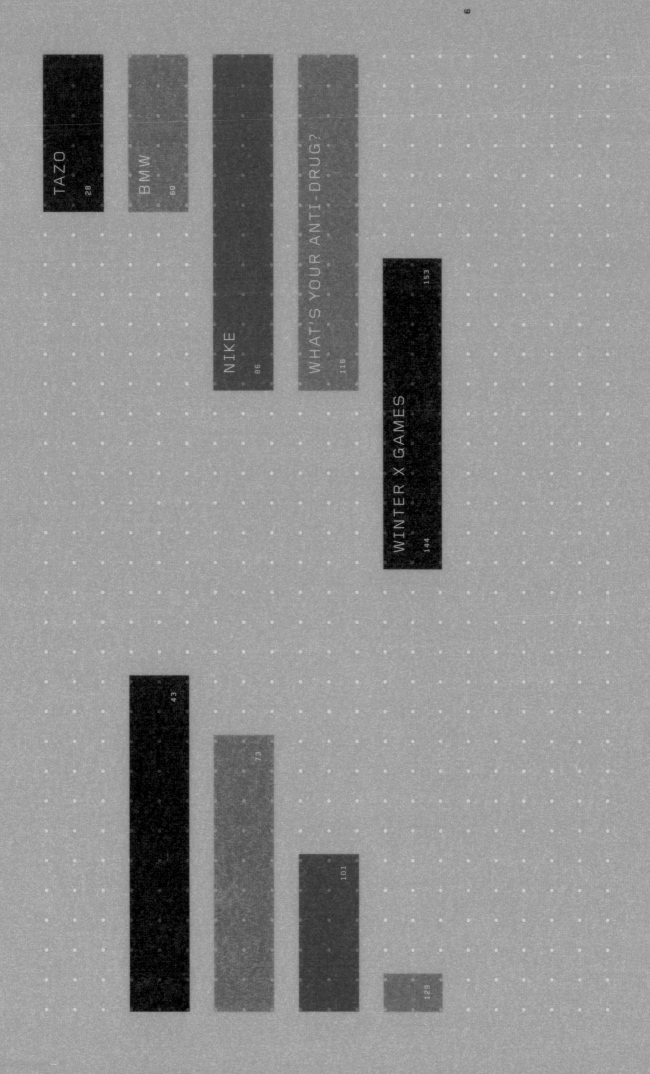

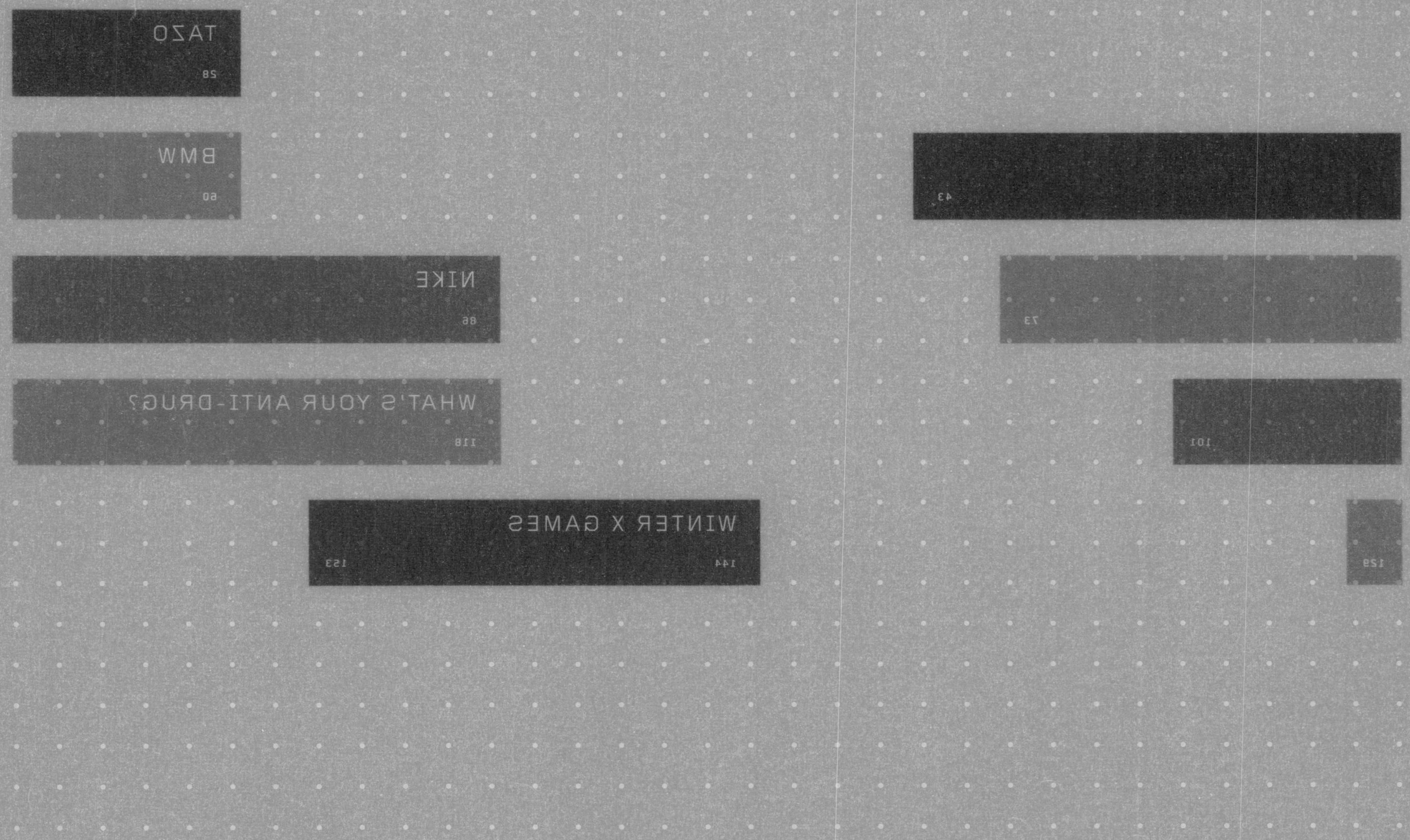

WINTER X GAMES

WHAT'S YOUR ANTI-DRUG?

NIKE

BMW

TAZO

PREFACE

JOE DUFFY chairman [DUFFY & PARTNERS]

Let's all admit that the number of impressions we make is far less important than the quality of impression we make. Simple repetition of a brand message does not break through the clutter, it only joins it. So how do we penetrate today's visual mélange and engage our audiences? I believe we must be repetitive instead in our daily pursuit of excellence and consistency.

This book is a celebration of marketing communications that work together to achieve greatness. I've chosen a handful of brands that are shepherded by some of the industry's leading thinkers. Their work represents communication that is not only at the highest end of creativity, it's also earning results in the marketplace.

This book is a celebration of marketing communications that work together to achieve greatness, I've chosen a handful of brands that are shaped by some of the industry's highest thinkers. Their work represent communication that is not only leading at the highest of creativity, it's also earning results in the marketplace.

We must not ignore this work. It refuses to be unseen or unheard of. It taunts us with its brilliance, its charm and, to the approval of anyone footing the bill, its proven effectiveness.

We must not ignore this work. If it refuses to be unseen,
it taunts us with its brilliance, its charm and, and to the
bill, its proven effectiveness

or to unhead of anyone
or uproval

Let the contents of this book serve as proof of the extraordinary impression that seamless marketing communication has on our audience, our culture, our industry, and on the business of our clients. Great work and great results are inextricably linked. And any brand created with this rule in mind will live to be a truly exceptional brand.

contents of this book serve as proof of the extraordinary impression
that seamless marketing communication has on our audience, our
culture, our industry, and on the business of our clients. Great work
and great results are inextricably linked. And any brand created with
this rule in mind will live to be a truly exceptional brand.

THE BAHAMAS

CHALLENGE How do we differentiate the Bahamas from all the other sun and sand destinations and keep people coming back again and again? And how do you build an identity system that integrates the public and private sectors?

SOLUTION Celebrate the culture, the people and the many unique God-given assets of the islands.

RESULT Bahamians have embraced and rallied behind the new branding approach, customer service ratings are improving and bookings are up. Competitive Caribbean destinations are scrambling to respond.

VINCENT VANDERPOOL-WALLACE director general [BAHAMAS MINISTRY OF TOURISM]

DAN OLSON creative director [DUFFY & PARTNERS]

TODD RIDDLE group creative director [FALLON WORLDWIDE]

TOM KUNAU lead producer [FALLON WORLDWIDE]

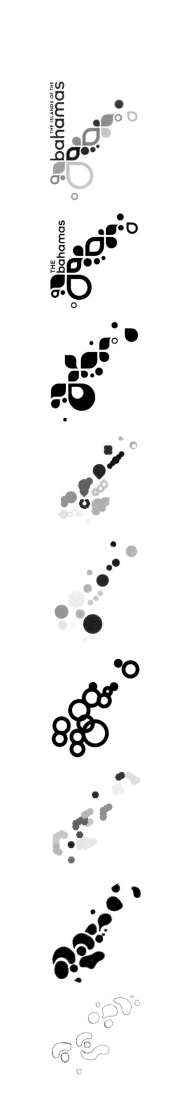

JOE DUFFY **Would you please outline what the Ministry of Tourism's expectations were for this effort?**

VINCENT VANDERPOOL-WALLACE Our brief was very simply to tell the world who we really are as opposed to allowing the world to continue to perceive us in a way that is very limiting and doesn't address the true potential of the Islands of the Bahamas. We wanted to show that the Bahamas are a very important entity within the region and we wanted to give each individual island its own identity as well.

When we saw the solution, we looked at it and it seemed obvious.

DUFFY **Was this the first time that you called upon one group to attend to design, advertising and the Web site?**

VANDERPOOL-WALLACE This is the first time that we were totally committed to doing something — whatever it was — in a fully integrated effort. That was really the second challenge of this assignment. We had never found ourselves satisfied with any one organization taking on the entire responsibility.

DUFFY **Dan, have you ever had an assignment where you had to develop an identity that could represent so many things?**

DAN OLSON This was new territory for us. Not only were we designing a new identity for an entire country, the system had to be incredibly hard working. It had to represent the country and the individual islands, as well as some very important private sector groups. We had to build the mark so that you could pull it apart in nearly 20 different ways. It was really an ambitious thing to try to accomplish.

DUFFY **Is designing an identity for a country different than designing an identity for a truck or a line of clothes or anything else?**

OLSON The approach and the process really aren't much different. It's about trying to get at the core of what something is — whether it's a country or a car company or a flower shop down the street. It's about trying to find tangible ways to bring the intangible to life. It's about taking all the words and all the visuals, and marrying them up in a way that becomes symbolic and telegraphic.

DUFFY **Talk a little bit about the idea of island hopping and how that came to be.**

TODD RIDDLE The Ministry of Tourism felt that the best way for us to know the Bahamas was for us to experience them for ourselves. So they invited us all down there for ten days or so. We spent our time in planes and on boats, going from one location to another. We met tour guides, pub owners, hotel workers — many, many people — and they all told us that the thing that separated the Bahamas from other Caribbean destinations was how great the people are. They wanted us to experience their kindness, their hospitality; these were the experiences that became the groundwork of the idea.

It was an idea that transcended all communication platforms. And it was really the same idea that spawned the identity at the very beginning of our efforts in the pitch for the business. The Web site is actually an extension of tv, so you go deeper and deeper and deeper. The identity is like the doorway to multiplicity — all these different destinations.

TOM KUNAU It's a situation that begged for an interactive experience. We wanted others to experience what we did, so we built an online island-hopping tool. It allows users to go through a virtual experience of dropping onto an island, hearing the waves, feeling sand between your toes and squinting into the sun.

Berry Islands

Abaco

Grand Bahama

Bimini

Andros

Nassau
Paradise Island

Exuma

Eleuthera
Harbour Island

Long Island

Cat Island

DUFFY **One of the most impressive things is seeing the whole campaign come to life and how the identity weaves in and out of each of the pieces of communications in a seamless framework. Was that something that was pre-described at the outset?**

OLSON The work evolved to that place because the mark seemed to make so much sense. It was such a good statement about the islands. And it became integral to how other things came to life.

RIDDLE We started out somewhat structured and it became less structured as we worked. Now it's very fluid, to the point where if we're talking about an identity change or a radio spot or anything, we all talk about it together and think about how each element affects everything else.

DUFFY **Can there be a formula for delivering this all-encompassing brand experience?**

KUNAU It's about keeping the communication open. As we traveled, we talked a lot. We sketched and shared ideas with people from all disciplines. We all had a common understanding of the challenges. And that communication continued after we got home.

OLSON It was a small and focused team. We shared the same goals. We had high aspirations. Many of us experienced the islands together, for the first time. That made a big difference. We shared a lot of the same assets. Ultimately, we galvanized our ideas and got on the same page right from the start.

RIDDLE It was like on the MTV show, "The Real World." We all lived together for about ten days and we got to know not only the Bahamas but each other as well. Looking back, it is a great way to work on any project because you get to know the people you're with.

island hopping

San Salvador

Acklins
Crooked Island

Inagua

Mayaguana

A friend of mine has a daughter and she said to me once, "I never really could get to know you until we played together." What a great insight from that child. That was the key here, too. We got to play together and it was a great working relationship with our own team and with the client.

DUFFY **Talk a little more about the role of the client in all of this.**

KUNAU They are an extremely intelligent, articulate, knowledgeable and engaged group of people. And they consistently give us quite a bit of leeway.

VANDERPOOL-WALLACE To be honest, we were a skeptical

group. We had given this brief to a number of other groups before, and we were very surprised to have gotten so close the first time out of the gate with this group. And then we got more and more excited about the prospect of making it work. I think one of the hallmarks of any good work is that people begin to see the solutions before they are explained to them. I think that is critically important because if you have to go through a great deal of explanation about what it is you are trying to tell someone, then almost by definition it is a failure. We knew it was right when we found ourselves making recommendations to the agency team about various parts of the campaign.

We knew they were onto something because we began to

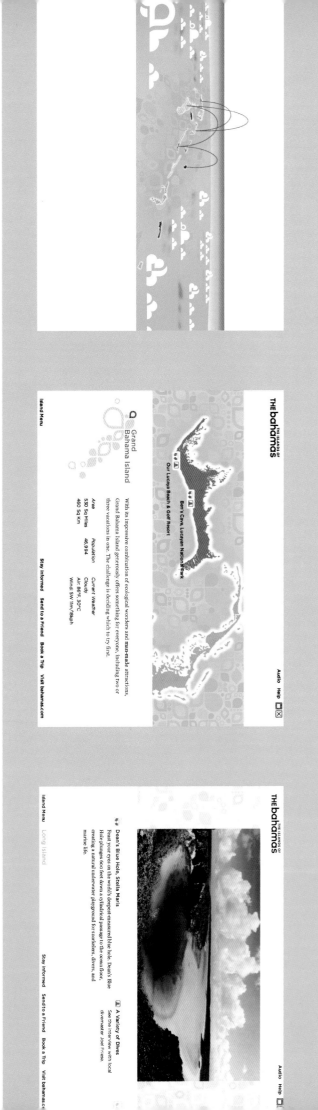

see for ourselves of how it worked and how it was going to play out. With that, we continued to challenge them to do more and make it even better.

RIDDLE I give them a lot of credit for having that vision and sticking with it. It was challenging. It hadn't changed for them in years. And we worked at it for a while before everything came together. They knew they wanted to be different — from what they had been doing and what so many others in the category were doing — but they didn't know exactly what things would look like.

They took a tremendous leap of faith and put a lot of trust in us and said, "You know you guys are the pros. We don't

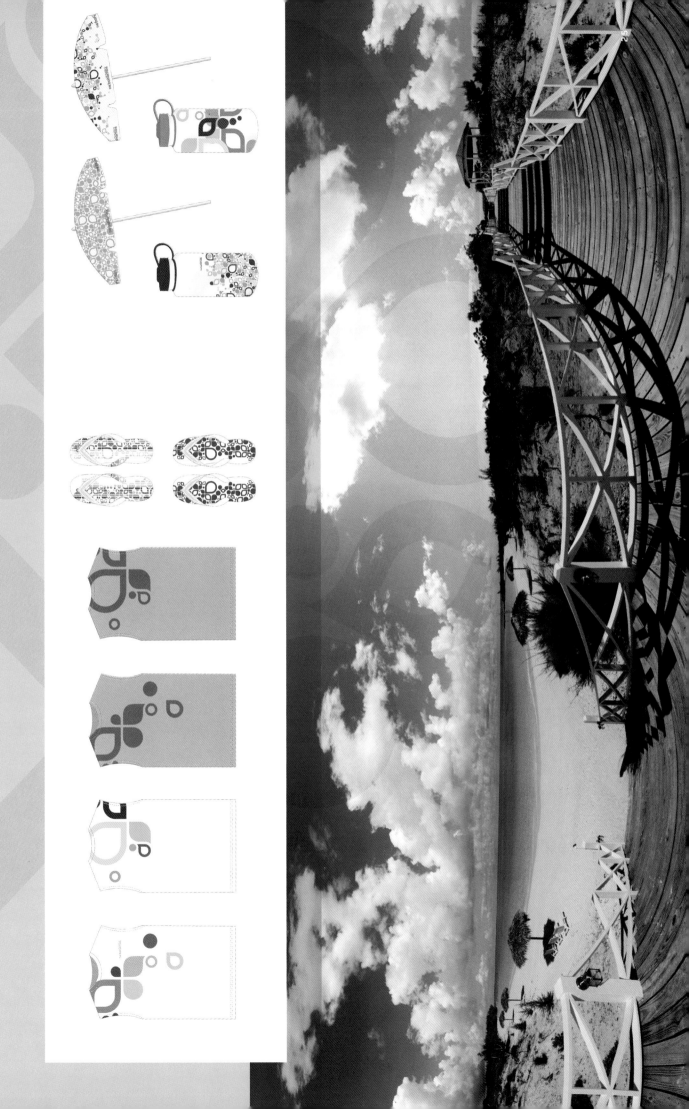

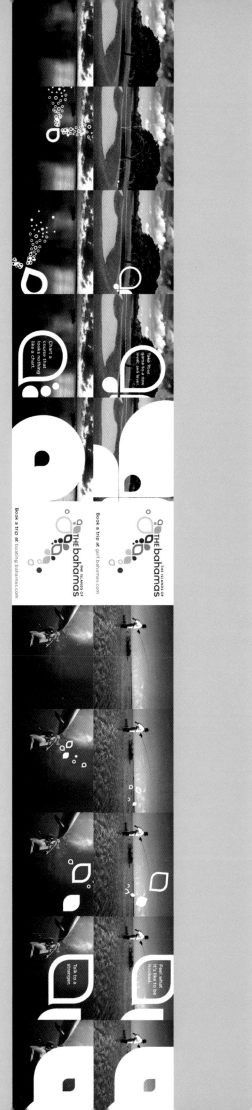

know what exactly it is that we want, but it needs to be out of the box and bold." They deserve a lot of credit because they challenged us every step of the way and really wanted us to rise up to that challenge with every single thing we did and continue to do.

DUFFY **What has been the best part of this experience?**

OLSON   I always enjoy the competitive nature of a pitch and watching people come together to get something so significant done in such a short period of time.

RIDDLE   The best part of the project is seeing it all come together. It's like building a rocket ship as it's taking off. It takes a lot of trust and a lot of different people across a lot of platforms to make the vision come to life. It's very, very complex.

VANDERPOOL-WALLACE   Without a doubt, the highlight for me was the first reveal of the identity. It was an "A-ha!" moment. And at the same time, we felt like we had to contain ourselves because we didn't want to let everybody know that we were so excited about it.

The biggest surprise to me was the speed in which the work was embraced, and how it was almost unanimous. This has been a primary objective of mine for over ten years. It's been a long quest and a tremendous personal accomplishment so far.

Official Tourism Website of
The Islands of The Bahamas

My Bahamas / Sign up to save, edit, share and print your vacation plans.

About The Bahamas   Plan a Trip   Book a Trip   Events   Weather

THE ISLANDS OF
THE bahamas

Island Hopping.
Day 2. Follow in no one's footsteps.

Vacation Planning Tools

○ Start with our Vacation Guide
○ Create an itinerary with My Bahamas
○ Book a trip online

The Bahamas Experience

○ All Abaco Sailing Regatta
○ Junkanoo
○ Andros Goombay Festival

Vacation Packages

○ The Hemingway
○ The Honeymooner
○ Stella Maris Resort Club

See All Packages

Search

Bahamas Island Hop Tour℠
Download and explore panoramic views
and video interviews from 22 locations.

© 2003 The Islands Of The Bahamas // Contact Us // Privacy // Site Map

---

THE ISLANDS OF
THE bahamas

My Bahamas / Sign up to save, edit, share and print your vacation plans.

About The Bahamas   Plan a Trip   Book a Trip   Events   Weather

Day 4.
Straw Market.
You know it. You know
what it is not without
it on the trip.

Shopping
Kinds of Diving
Dive Shops
Gallery
Related Islands
Where to Stay
Travel Tips

Bring an appetite for authenticity. Today's Bahamians continue
the tradition of early island natives by using local resources to
create distinct items that reflect their heritage. Straw Markets
reveal foods, spices, ceramics, crafts, art, and music.

The Bahamas Experience

○ Bahamas Island Hop (SM)
○ Abaco Adventures Ferry Schedule
○ Great Abaco Triathlon

Vacation Packages

○ The Hemingway
○ The Honeymooner
○ Stella Maris Resort Club

See All Packages

Add to My Bahamas
Sign up to save, edit,
share and print your
vacation plans.

Send this page to a friend

Search

© 2003 The Islands of The Bahamas // Contact Us // Privacy // Site Map

---

THE ISLANDS OF
THE bahamas

My Bahamas / Sign up to save, edit, share and print your vacation plans.

About The Bahamas   Plan a Trip   Book a Trip   Events   Weather

Grand Bahama
Island

Cities
Airports
Diving
Fishing
Golf Courses
National Parks

About the Island
History
What to Do
Where to Stay
Packages
Events
Map
Getting There
Getting Around
Travel Tips
Gallery

Search

© 2003 The Islands of The Bahamas // Contact Us // Privacy // Site Map

---

THE ISLANDS OF
THE bahamas

My Bahamas / Sign up to save, edit, print your vacation plans.

About The Bahamas   Plan a Trip   Book a Trip   Events   Weather

Book a Trip
Packages/Hotel/Flight/Cars
Choose a package type:
Flight and hotel

Departing from:

Depart:
10/22/03
Morning

Going to:

Return:
10/22/03
Morning

Adults   Seniors   Children
2   0   0

More package destinations

Search

Day 1
6,000 rooms.
Beginning your
approach.

The vacation plans you put into motion now are guaranteed to stop
you in your tracks when you see the beauty and opportunity awaiting
you in The Bahamas. Choose from packages, flights, hotels, and cars
to book your trip on bahamas.com.

Did you already book a trip on bahamas.com?
Please sign in to access your account.

Sign in.

© 2003 The Islands of The Bahamas // Contact Us // Privacy // Site Map

---

THE ISLANDS OF
THE bahamas

THE ISLANDS OF
THE bahamas

k a trip at fishing.bahamas.com

k a trip at diving.bahamas.com

TAZO

CHALLENGE The introduction of a new brand of tea to the crowded beverage category in a country where tea was seen as passé.

SOLUTION Find new ways to tell a story, because traditional mass advertising seemed counter to the brand's positioning; create intrigue; and build the highest-quality connection at every point—product, branding, and merchandising design.

RESULT Tazo—a brand that developed instant authenticity and even a passionate consumer following.

STEVE SANDSTROM *creative director and partner* [SANDSTROM DESIGN]

STEVE SMITH *founder* [TAZO]

JOE DUFFY Can you start at the beginning? Tell us about how Tazo started and who was involved.

STEVE SMITH It started with a framework of concepts and images for a new tea retailer. The working title was Elixir. The idea was that it would be an "elixir bar" and it would have a Merlin-meets-Marco-Polo feel to it. That was the starting point. When I realized I wasn't going to do retail, I used that same platform and started working on some in-store merchandising ideas. I was trying to get the merchandising side of the business defined because I felt that too few people look at that. It's critical to look at how to carve out your space in a retail store so that it's really compelling to the consumer.

I was working on the idea with my partner, Steve Lee. Steve Sandoz was helping us, too, and it was at least a month before we even had a brand name. At one point early in the process, I said, "Do you think Steve Sandstrom would look at this, too?" Sandoz said, "Yeah, I think so." And so we met with the folks at Sandstrom. There was an immediate connection, and we decided after that initial meeting to move forward.

STEVE SANDSTROM When they came over, there were three Steves — Steve Sandoz, Steve Lee and Steve Smith — meeting with me, a fourth Steve. Something in the tea leaves, I guess. That's where we started. Four Steves and an idea to come up with a new kind of tea.

SMITH We asked ourselves, what if Marco Polo met Merlin? It would be a little bit of magic, a little bit of mystery, and a little bit of history.

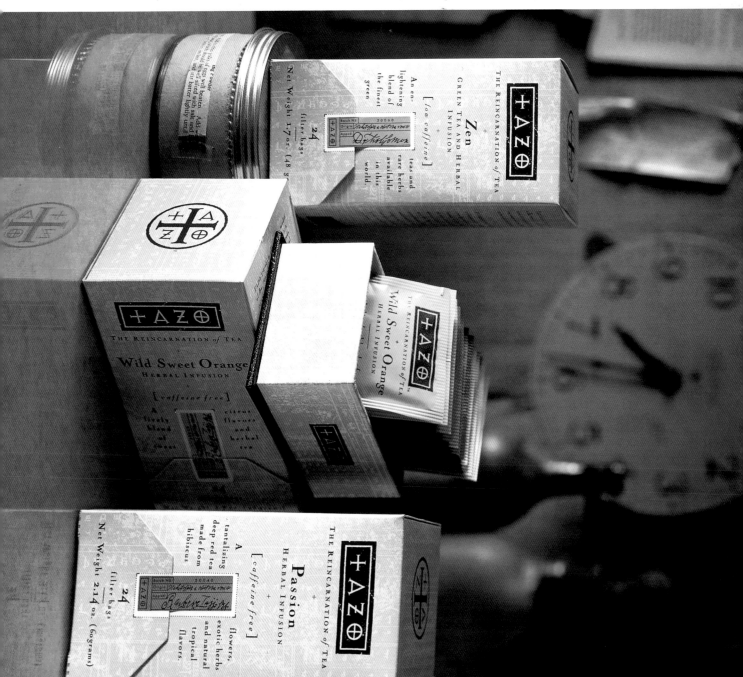

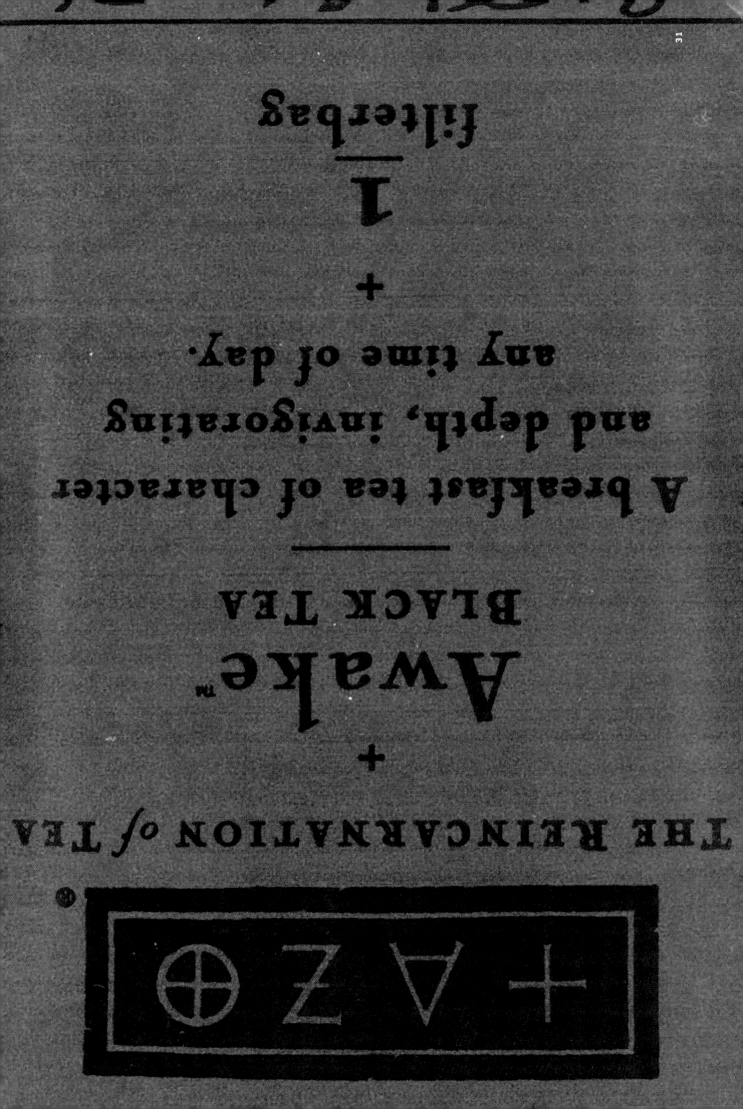

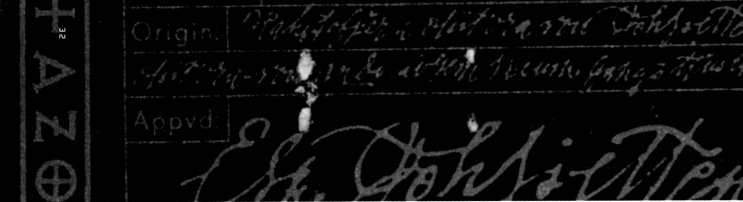

The business goal was to make the best tea we could possibly make. To not cut any corners. And to get people engaged with tea in a way that they hadn't been before. From the very beginning, we wanted to change the whole idea of tea — that tea was boring, dull, stuffy. These were the myths about the category at the time. They were well deserved in the U.S., based on the way tea had been offered up to consumers in the past. The challenge was to create a new brand architecture, a new voice, a whole new approach to tea. We wanted to create something that was fresh and untried. That's where we started.

DUFFY That's one of the things that's so interesting about this brand — the marriage of a great business idea with a remarkably artistic presentation. There aren't many good examples of brands that walk the fine line between being something absolutely right for the marketplace and something that attracts the attention and admiration of creative people. Can you tell a little more about how this concept of Marco Polo meets Merlin came to life as Tazo?

SANDSTROM Well, we didn't really have any products. We didn't even have a name at that point. We had four Steves in

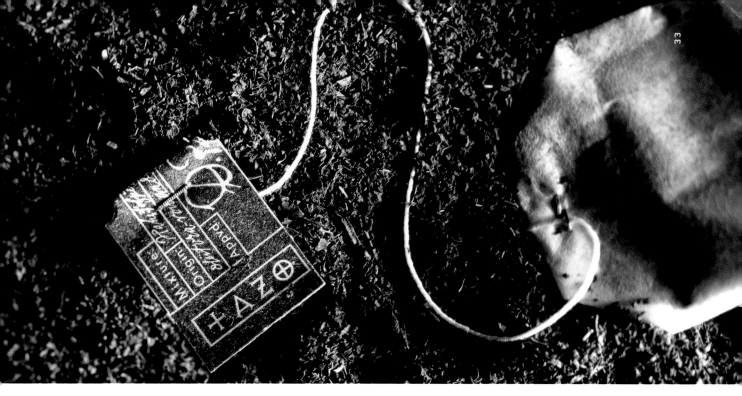

REFRESH   TAZO CHAI   ZEN

a room, and they all wanted to start a tea company based on Marco Polo meets Merlin. We set out to achieve something with that sort of looseness.

DUFFY Sounds like one of those opportunities where you had a great team and a fabulous brief — an inspired vision with room to roam.

SMITH Absolutely. The parameters we gave ourselves were that we didn't want to appear frivolous. We needed to make sure that the product was really special. And we wanted there to be discoveries in the brand that would tie it all together

into a story bigger than the tea and the merchandising and the packaging.

We believed these things would make a difference and that people would be interested in them. Also, at about the time we were developing Tazo, we knew that different feelings about quality and value were starting to emerge in our society.

SANDSTROM So that was the platform. From there, Sandoz went off to think of a name. We wanted to make something up. We didn't want it to sound too American. Tea leaves

The Tazo logo is set in Exocet, a font created by Jon Barnbrook after studying design at both St. Martin's School of Art and the Royal College of Art in London.

SMITH Sandoz finally came up with the name, "Taza." When he told us about it, he said, "It's got a z in it, it's four letters, it's two vowels..." From there, it manipulated itself into Tazo. About a week passed, and people started asking me, "What does 'Tazo' mean?" So I talked to Sandoz and told him we needed to search to see if there was any meaning in any language or culture associated with the name. That's where Steve started uncovering all of these oddball facts. Fact and fiction started blending together. And that's where it all began.

DUFFY It looks cool. It's short and simple.

SANDSTROM It's short, and it's Tazo. It's just one of those things that's good. It doesn't sound American. We were fortunate that we found the word only in three or four dialects. And it's always meant something positive. In one Romanian dialect it means "river of life."

don't grow here anyway, so why should it be from here? We worked closely and very collaboratively throughout the whole creative process.

SMITH We really did. We talked through the whole process and found ourselves in a kind of a cabinet mentality during creative sessions. If one of us felt very strongly about a direction, that's the direction it would go.

DUFFY I think an important ingredient to highly successful brands is this process of collaboration that includes the client. How did that work?

SANDSTROM Well, it helped that Steve [Smith] is a very creative guy. Even as the client and as more of a business mind, he's very entrepreneurial. And, he's fascinated with the creative process. He respects it and allows it to happen. That makes him a really great client.

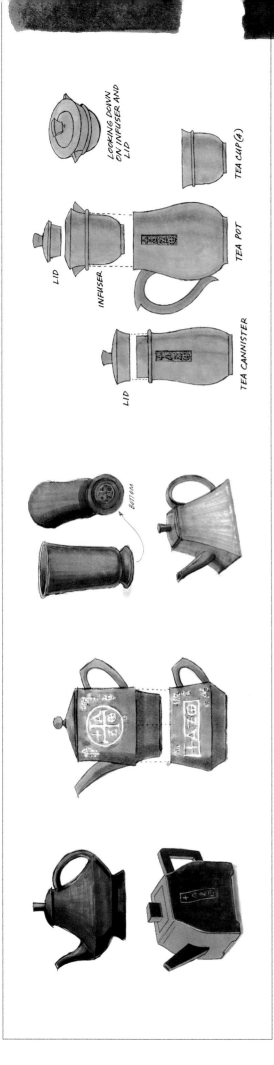

LOOKING DOWN ON INFUSER AND LID

TEA CUP (4)

LID
INFUSER
TEA POT

TEA CANNISTER
LID

BOTTOM

SMITH It was maybe a few weeks later that we were talking about the Dalai Lama, and the concept of the reincarnation of tea emerged from a conversation that Steve Lee and I were having. We talked to Sandoz about it. At the time, he was toying with the soul of tea. I guess I thought that was a little pompous. But as it happened, it just worked. It really was incredibly organic and probably the best collaboration of creativity I could ever imagine. Who knew it would connect like it did? The whole notion of us trying to recreate tea in the American mentality — trying to reincarnate — was kind of an interesting idea. Something old that's new again.

DUFFY It gave you the opportunity to create a brand with an authentic story. In our work, we find that's important for consumers so they can connect with something real.

SANDSTROM Exactly. And that concept of authenticity — with a slight twist — drove everything we did. Everybody loved

how the concept was evolving, and I went away to figure out something for a logo. Finally I stumbled across that Exocet font that Jonathan Barnbrook had designed, and that was it. There was an alchemist symbol look to it.

DUFFY What I love about it is that it reads clearly, yet when you look at it with a different set of eyes, it almost seems that there aren't letters there. It's symbols and letters simultaneously.

SANDSTROM The fact that it is full of geometry and that it could be a symbol before a letter seemed to fit. I basically took those letterforms and then roughed them up as if they were stone rubbings. That was it.

SMITH Beyond being a collaborative process, it was really organic. The creation of the logo was an evolutionary process. When we finally got to a solution, I painted it on our van.

Then, a few weeks later, I had to go back and add "the reincarnation of tea." We also had to add the cross to the Z. It wasn't there initially. And then the cross on the O. I really struggled with the cross on the O. I loved the cross on the Z, but I didn't like the cross on the O so much. But, as I said, we worked like a cabinet, and in the end the strongest feeling won out.

DUFFY In terms of developing the voice for the brand, the reincarnation of tea is obviously a big part of it. Can you talk about how it developed?

SMITH For me, I could envision this multicultural mélange of experiences coming together — borrowing from the Asian culture and the Indian and African cultures — to create this new tea experience. But I couldn't, and I didn't, envision the total brand voice. Sandoz really came up with that, and it was this voice that started to define where the brand was going.

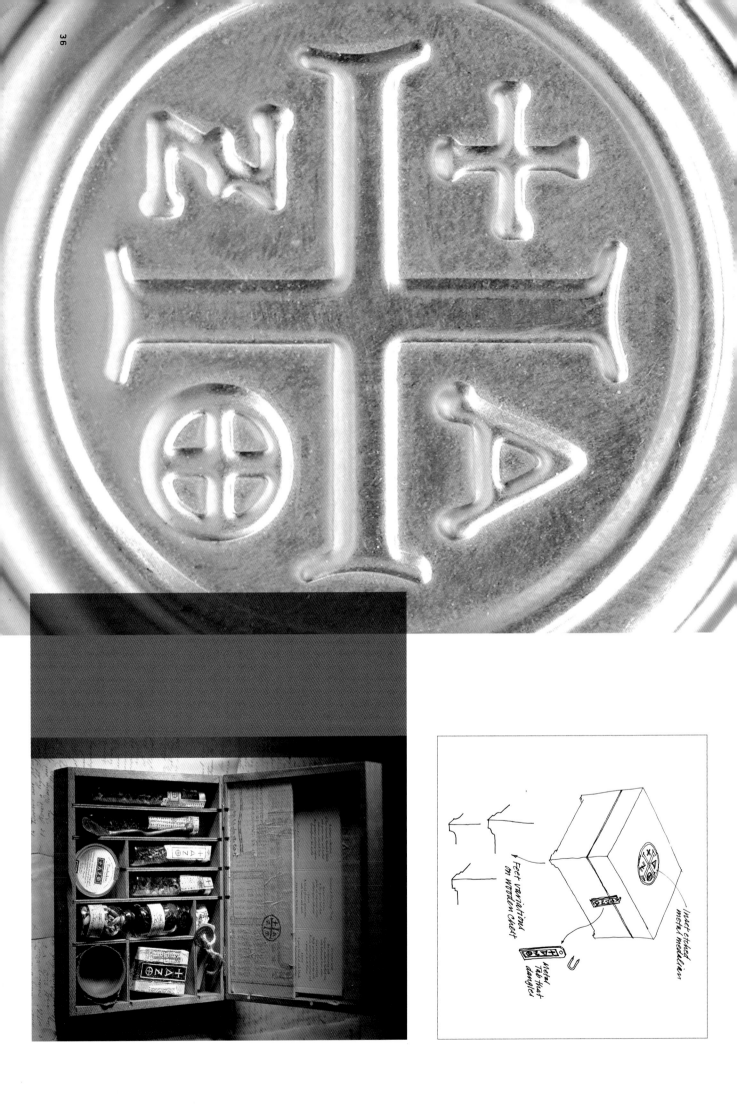

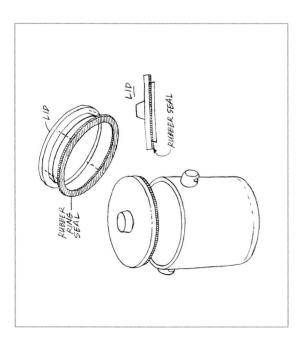

RUBBER RING SEAL

LID

LID

RUBBER SEAL

80mm

64 mm

Much of it started with the tag line, "The reincarnation of tea." We started to design the packaging language as if it were from another place and time.

As this was all happening, we didn't have much manpower at Tazo, and I knew I needed to deal with the realities of focusing on issues like getting a product out the door. Because of the timing, we had to develop packaging before we even had a product. So, if you can imagine, I developed eight different blends based on rough ingredient lists and a sentence or two about what they'd taste like.

From there I handed it over to Sandoz, and he continued to build the Tazo voice by describing the blends and naming them in a Tazo kind of way with mood state names, like "Zen" and "Calm," "Passion" and "Refresh," and others that fit our brand position. We made film and plates and were printing packaging before we had the product. It was like we

were walking on a tightrope. Then I started working on the formulas in earnest. To be honest, I was really concerned because I knew I'd have to create a blend that would go into this package and deliver upon the promise it was making. I wasn't sure I could live up to that.

SANDSTROM At the core of everything, I believe it was the respect and trust that we had for each other and our respective skills and talents that made this whole thing as powerful as it is.

Steve [Smith] said to me, "When you showed me the boxes, I knew I had to step up; I knew I had to make these formulas the best they could possibly be. They just had to be." If there was anything, it was their trust in us as creative partners and our belief in them as clients — their knowledge of tea and business, and their abilities to accomplish anything they wanted to accomplish — that made this whole thing work.

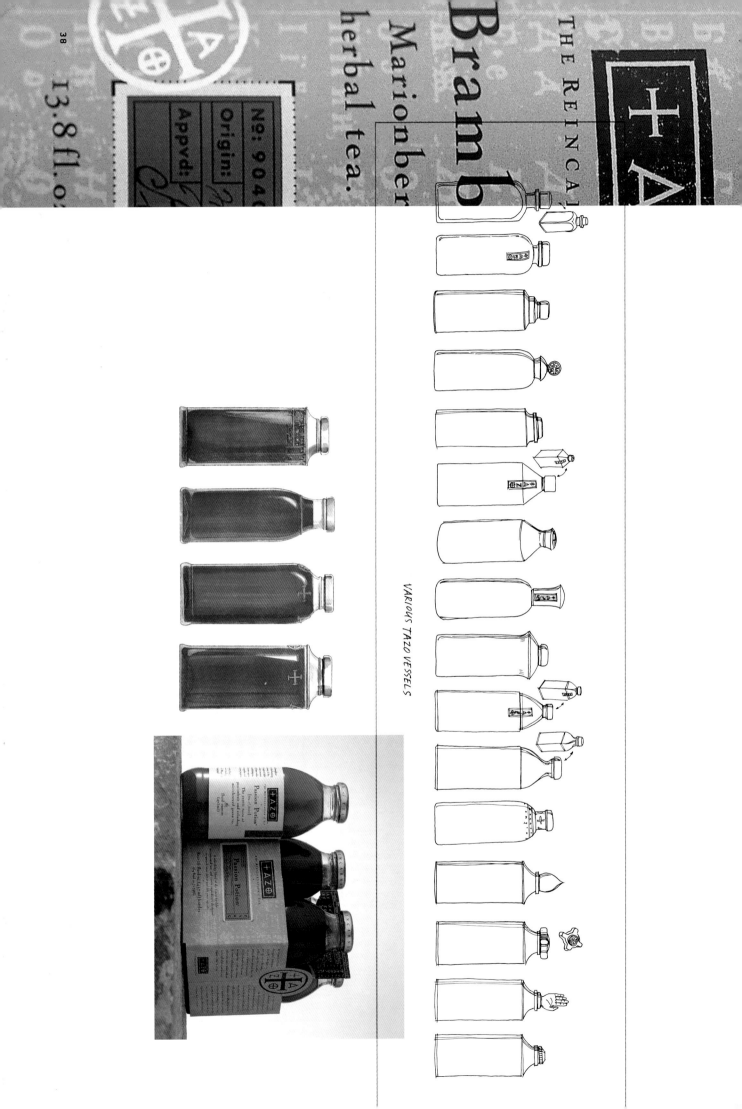

13.8 fl. oz

Nº: 9040
Origin:
Appvd:

herbal tea.

Marionber

Bram b

THE REINCA

VARIOUS TAZO VESSELS

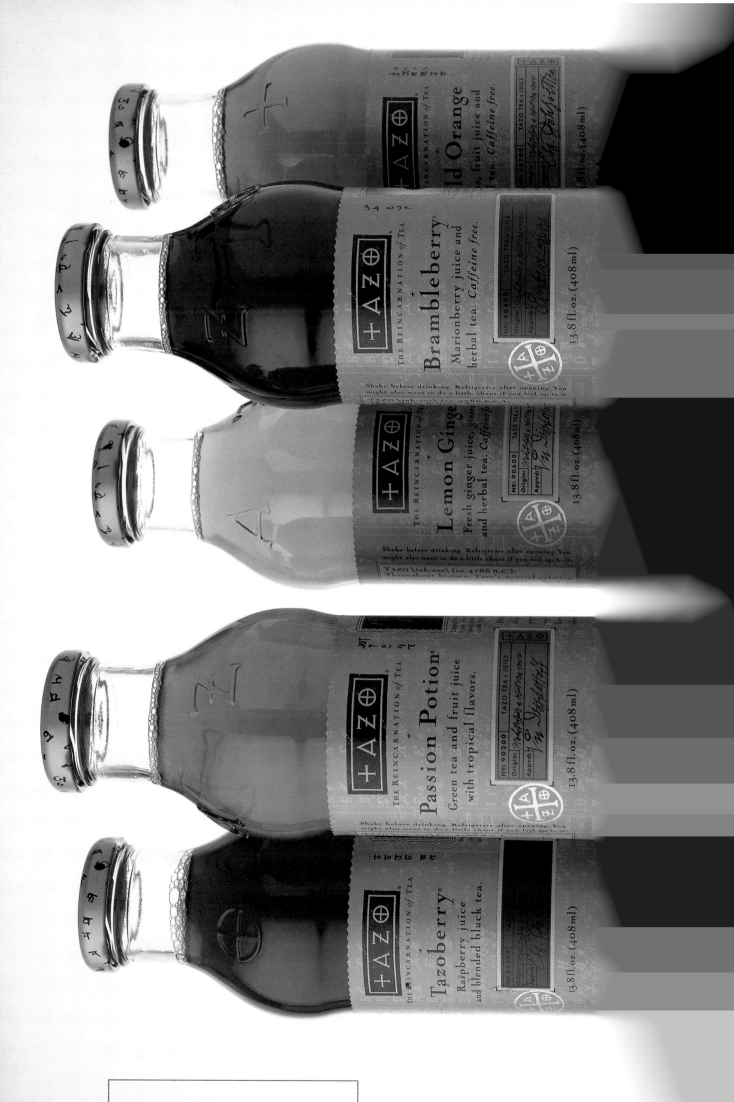

DUFFY It is very obvious that you all cared deeply about what you were doing. What I usually find is that if people take care in the presentation of their brand, that care is usually representative of how they develop their product as well. And that's a formula for success.

SANDSTROM I'd add one more thing that made this so successful, and it's a willingness to take a risk. They were willing to take a risk with a made-up name — one that's not easy to pronounce — and a whole new way to present a brand. I thought it was a risk, too. But I knew it had to be.

I expected the public to think it was 2/3 cool and maybe 1/3 crazy. It was probably more like 85% and 15%. I thought there was just enough edge to put it at risk. But it's exactly the sort of edge that makes people more excited about it. They love what looked different. They thought it looked real. Today, consumers are passionate about it.

DUFFY Advertising efforts have been minimal and focused in small space ads in vertical publications. Is that purposeful?

SANDSTROM It is. Doing advertising was something we thought would be fun, but we also knew we had to make sure that the brand didn't become too slick, too polished, too good. And the timing had to be right. We had to achieve a certain amount of success, of mystique, before we could be sure that advertising wouldn't become counterproductive or dangerous. We didn't want marketing to harm the brand, if you know what I mean.

SMITH Exactly. And the general idea of the brand and the voice was to try to get anybody who picks up this package to read further, to engage in an intimate way.

DUFFY You did a great job of nourishing the mystique.

SANDSTROM It works so well because we have public favor and the resulting word of mouth. There have been thousands of letters written to Tazo every week. We've been able to make a really amazing personal connection with people. Somebody once wrote a letter that said, "We're thinking about naming our pet llama 'Tazo.' Is that O.K.?"

DUFFY Have you saved any classic letters?

SANDSTROM There are boxes of letters. Steve [Smith] and I had to give a presentation to a marketing group one time, and he called me and said, "I don't know what to say." I told him, "Just start reading your mail." And that's what he did.

DUFFY Now Tazo is a big business. There's a partnership with Starbucks. How has that affected the brand and its mystique?

SANDSTROM That's a good question. And one that so many companies face. How do you grow your distribution and exposure and not ruin an image that's been built by being special and unique versus mass? The biggest concern was the fact that Starbucks is a coffee company. Would they respect and understand the Tazo brand and philosophy? Starbucks has been good about respecting, maintaining, and growing our brand. They've developed new products like Chai tea and the Tazoberry Freezes, which have helped the brand and the business. They understand that it's important for the Tazo brand to continue to be its own thing.

DUFFY It's a never-ending job, isn't it? To build, protect, and nurture a brand?

SANDSTROM It is. And it's important to have the right relationships at the right levels. There needs to be a shared understanding of where a brand is coming from, as well as an understanding of the risks, the rewards and the oppor-

Taste Tea?

It's a funny coincidence (maybe it's actually not that funny) but the way a real tea expert tastes tea is very similar to the way wine is savored and tasted. A tea is brewed, then allowed to cool and then slurped (it's called aspirating) to evaluate taste and aroma.

The way all Tazo tea tasters conduct a tea tasting involves a simple ritual. First, tea samples from the same region and harvest period are placed side by side in special tasting pots. A predetermined amount of tea is placed in each pot. The pots are filled with boiling water and allowed to brew for five minutes. This brewed tea (or liquor) is drained into individual porcelain bowls, allowing the leaves to remain in the pot. The tea is then evaluated for aroma, strength, top note (or dominant flavor) and aftertaste.

When conducting your own tea tasting, remember to use similar sized cups, put the same amount of tea in each cup (approximately one teaspoon or one filterbag), and brew for the appropriate time (5 min for blacks and herbals and 3 to 4 minutes for greens and oolongs). These are the qualities you should consider:

ASTRINGENCY This is a puckery characteristic in tea. Astringent teas tend to leave a dry taste in the mouth as an aftertaste.

BRIGHT The refers to a pleasant, almost fresh baked aroma.

BRISK A fresh, light and lively taste.

BRISK A tea of light, fresh taste with high astringency.

CHARACTER This refers to a quality that is characteristic of the specific region the tea came from.

COLOURY Good quality teas with a rich, deep red, amber or copper color and good strength.

LIQUOR The color and strength of tea within the cup.

MOJO The vibe the tea gives off if you happen to be the least bit psychic.

PUFFINESS How well the tea goes with pastries or desserts.

PERSONALITY Does the tea respect the property of others and follow directions?

To describe the flavor of a particular tea it is helpful to identify tastes and aromas by associating them with other foods, beverage or scents you are familiar with such as fruits, nuts, flowers or spices. You should also consider the mouth-feel of the tea and the overall fullness.

WHAT FORMS DOES TAZO TAKE?

TAZO COMES IN many forms, all of them delicious. Fresh brewed Tazo may be created from filterbag or full leaf teas. In either style you'll find the best teas, the most intriguing flavors and the most captivating experiences. Listed below are some of the flavors available.

TAZO FILTERBAG TEAS:

AWAKE A robust blend of black teas from India and fragrant high-grown Ceylons that makes an excellent breakfast tea, but is delicious enough to drink all day long.

DARJEELING A blend of rare first and second flush organic Darjeeling teas.

EARL GREY A blend of fine black teas from India and Ceylon scented with the essence of pure Italian bergamot.

CITRON A light, aromatic tea with hints of lemon and orange essence.

ORGANIC TAZO CHAI A rich blend of tea and spices in the style of the hill dwellers of the Himalayas.

CHINA GREEN TIPS: A traditional Chinese green tea with a delicate bouquet, fresh taste and light green-colored liquor.

ZEN Chinese panfired green teas blended with mint and lemongrass.

OM Organically grown green Darjeeling teas lightly scented with cucumber and peach.

PASSION An herbal infusion of tropical hibiscus flowers with mango and passion fruit flavors.

REFRESH An herbal infusion of Northwest peppermint, spearmint and the sweet licorice taste of tarragon.

CALM An herbal infusion of chamomile blossoms, blackberry leaves and rose petals.

TAZO FULL LEAF TEAS:

Though Tazo filterbags are wonderful in every way and allow you to conveniently brew tea and everything else on the planet, for the ultimate tea experience we recommend you try Tazo full leaf teas. Full leaf Tazo, unencumbered by the restrictive dimensions of a filterbag, contain larger tea leaves, flowers and pieces of herbs and spices that unfold as the boiling water unlocks their flavor and mystery. At the end of a cup also provides you with the materials necessary look into the future with a reading of your tea leaves.

FORMOSA OOLONG: An elegant tea that exists between green and black.

MAMBO A bold, red, tropical infusion.

TAZO CHAI

When Chai, the spicy, sweet tea drink of the Himalayas, was first created, it, and everything else on the planet, was made by hand. Tazo Chai still tastes as extraordinary as it did the day the first chai wallah set up his stall on the path to Muktinath. Containing rich black teas from North India and Sri Lanka blended with ginger, cinnamon, star anise, cloves and cardamom, Tazo Chai comes in full leaf and filterbag forms that may be sweetened and mixed with milk or a dairy substitute to taste. We also make a pre-blended form that only requires the addition of milk to prepare something extraordinary.

How is Tea Harvested?

DURING THE HARVEST period, known as the "flush", pluckers harvest the tender top two leaves and bud from each bush. New shoots are plucked every 7–10 days during the flush which may last up to 45 days.

An accomplished plucker can harvest 60 pounds of leaves in a day, an amazing feat when you consider the leaves are being plucked two and three at a time.

The plucked tea leaves are actually quite precious. In fact each pound will yield only about 50 cups of the delightful brew you're hopefully sipping right now.

During the Ch'in dynasty in China it was considered a crime to discuss Tazo unless you were actually drinking some of the precious substance. If you were caught "Tazoning", as it was called, the punishment was typically a week of work dusting the terracotta soldiers that had been sculpted to protect the emperor when he passed from this life.

GRADES OF TEA - The dried, fired tea is sorted by mechanical sifters with different sized screens into progressively smaller pieces. The larger the pieces, the more valuable the tea.
OP Orange Pekoe - full leaves
FOP Flowery Orange Pekoe - broken leaves
BOP Broken Orange Pekoe Fannings - even smaller pieces of the broken leaves
STOTF The Stuff That Falls On The Floor
ITC Inside The Gum Wrappers

How Does Tazo Blend Tea?

PIECING TOGETHER ANCIENT lore and artifacts, we now believe that Tazo was originally blended in an elaborate ceremony lasting upwards of 4 days and involving much dancing, music and the odd limbo contest.

Legend has it that both the French language and the tambourine may have been created during one of these Tazo-analias.

The Tazo you enjoy today is blended using what are thought to be many of the original formulas from the Tazo stone. The tea arrives at our blending facility from tea estates in foil-lined wooden chests, each filled with 50 kilos or so of tea. We take samples of these teas and categorize them according to their liquoring quality (which is the color, strength and taste quality of the brewed tea) and aroma. Using these samples we create a lab blend, make a few adjustments for flavor, chant a bit to get in touch with our inner tea shaman, and then begin carefully blending the teas in small batches.

In addition to pure blends of the world's finest high-grown teas, we often add other botanicals and spices to our tea blends to create a wide variety of unique tea drinking experiences. To create a full line of teas like this obviously takes more time and effort, but what's the point of having time if you don't use it to create something truly wonderful?

How Does Tazo Buy Tea?

IN KEEPING WITH the ancient traditions surrounding Tazo there is a bit of mystery involved in this process, but at the core is a very simple mission: Tazo always seeks to find and use the best teas available on the planet, regardless of cost or the difficulty we may have in obtaining them. This has been the case for untold centuries, since the times when a roving band of tea shaman circled the globe on camels and other large, ill-tempered beasts, searching for the specific teas necessary to create the magical perfection that is Tazo.

Tazo tea buyers visit the tea producing regions during the peak harvest periods to taste and make selections for the Tazo tea blends. We also have agents in Calcutta, Columbo and Shanghai who send us samples of available teas from the premier producing Tea Estates in each region. We always buy single estate teas, rather than teas blended at origin, which is the norm, and humid conditions can compromise quality.

We're picky. Only about one of ten we taste find their way into a Tazo blend. The things we consider are flavor, aroma and taste before choosing just the right teas to buy. We're much more concerned about how a tea tastes and smells than the trifling things like cost of ingredients.

After purchase, teas are shipped in their original wooden tea chests to Portland, OR, and blended there by our teamaker under the watchful eye of our Teamaster. By procuring tea this way, Tazo is always able to deliver a fresher product and maintain control over the taste and consistency of our blends.

As you might imagine, it takes a very discerning palate and a somewhat oversized bladder to do

How Do I Brew Tazo?

For each renewing cup of hot tea use one bag or one teaspoon (that's why they're called teaspoons) of full leaf tea to a tea infuser. Bring freshly drawn cold filtered water to a boil and pour into cup over tea. Allow black and herbal teas to steep for five minutes and allow green and oolong teas to steep for three to four minutes. Strain, remove bag or infuser and serve. Save the tea leaves to spread in your garden or toss as confetti.

To make iced tea, place two filterbags in an 8 ounce container and steep as above. Remove the bags and pour the hot tea into a tall glass filled with ice. Mmmm, good.

पिछले जन्म में, यही आपकी पसंदिता चाय थी ।
— In a past life, this was your favorite tea.

x5b

THANK YOU. IT WAS FREEZING IN HERE

HAVE ANOTHER IF I WERE YOU.

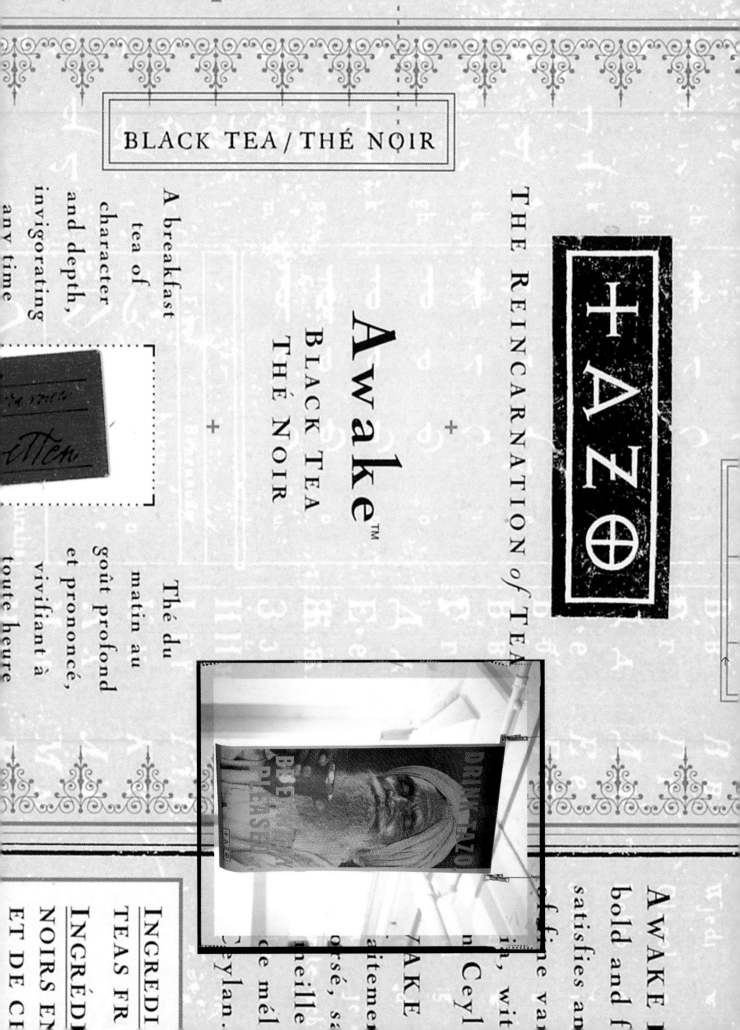

BLACK TEA / THÉ NOIR

THE REINCARNATION *of* TEA

TAZO

Awake™
BLACK TEA
THÉ NOIR

A breakfast tea of character and depth, invigorating any time

Thé du matin au goût profond et prononcé, vivifiant à toute heure

INGREDI
TEAS FR
INGRÉDI
NOIRS EN
ET DE CE

A WAKE
bold and f
satisfies an

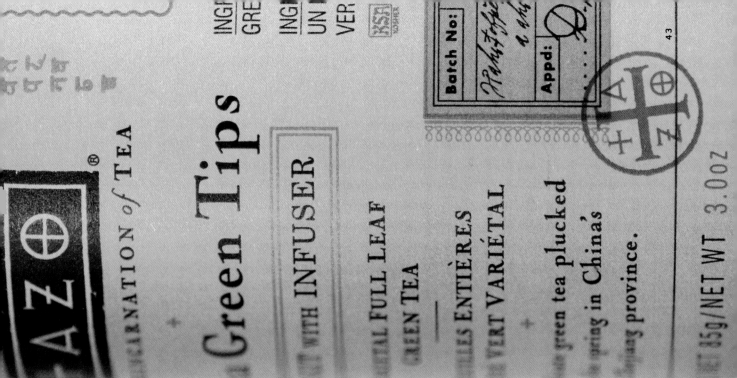

tunities. It is, and will always be, our job to be the brand evangelists.

SMITH And we also need to consider that, especially with the Starbucks partnership, we need to have broad appeal. We're not just trying to sell to a certain type of person or a specific demographic. It's a fine line to walk — to keep the mystique, while not coming across as being too niche or exclusive.

After all is said and done, it is satisfying to learn that our assumptions were accurate: that tea, done well, could be a good business and a cool brand. Even though we put the product into the market at a couple of dollars more per package, it looked like somebody shot a cannon through the shelf set in our first retail store. All the competitors were nicely faced up, but our boxes were turned on their sides with big gaping holes in the set. It was like that for the first few days, and we loved it.

When I'm in a bakery or a similar place, I'll see a little gray-haired lady walk in and overhear her ordering a cup of Zen or Envy or Om. I've heard it countless times. She knows what she's ordering when she's ordering Passion. And it's not something that she would usually say. But she's had this tea before. It crosses all sorts of demographic lines. I love that. It's really great.

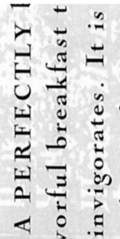

HARLEY-DAVIDSON

CHALLENGE The Harley-Davidson brand suffered from a bad image associated with notorious gangs of steel-horse outlaws.

SOLUTION A small group of visionaries within the company set out to rub leather-clad elbows at biker rallies, sniff out the genuine Harley-Davidson enthusiasts and refocus all communication on the one true reason the brand existed: the motorcycle.

RESULT Marking a new era in its brand's evolution, Harley-Davidson successfully wrestled its image away from roughnecks, while simultaneously leading a new generation of riding enthusiasts on a road trip that appears to have only on-ramps.

DANA ARNETT principal [VSA PARTNERS INC.]

TOM WATSON director of marketing [HARLEY-DAVIDSON MOTOR COMPANY]

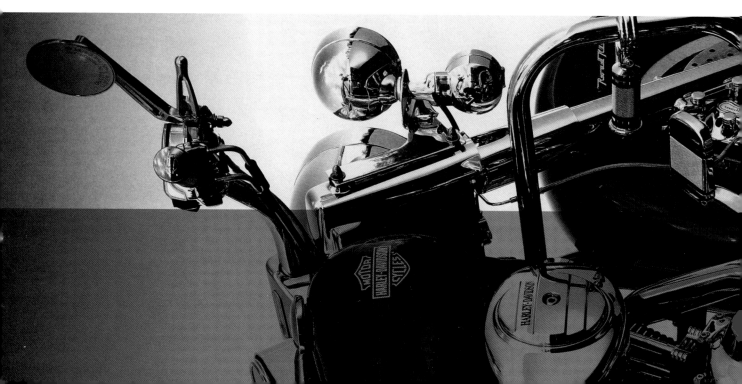

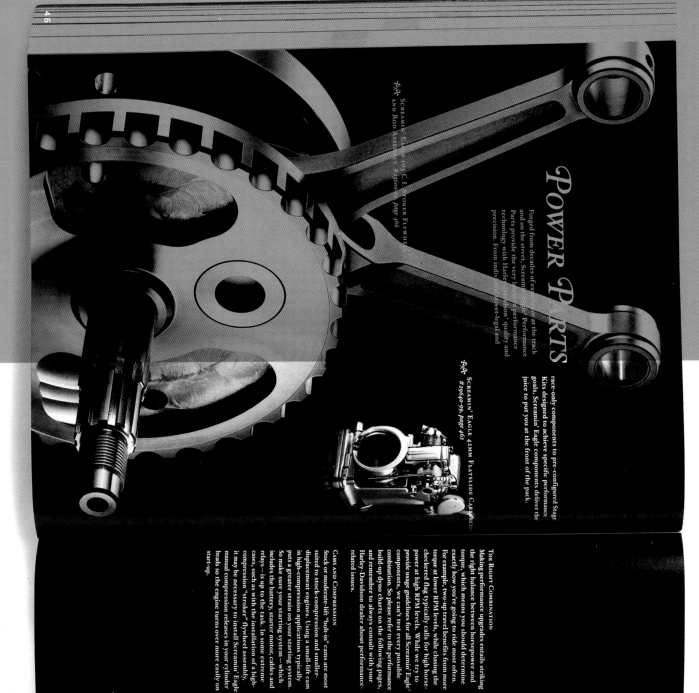

SCREAMIN' EAGLE 113 C.I. STROKER FLYWHEEL AND ROD ASSEMBLY, #23900-01, page 466

POWER PARTS

Forged from decades of experience at the track and on the street, Screamin' Eagle Performance Parts provide the very latest in performance technology with Harley-Davidson quality and precision. From individual street-legal and race-only components to pre-configured Stage Kits designed to achieve specific performance goals, Screamin' Eagle components deliver the juice to put you at the front of the pack.

SCREAMIN' EAGLE 42MM FLATSLIDE CARBURETOR, #29040-99, page 462

THE RIGHT COMBINATION

Making performance upgrades entails striking the right balance between horsepower and torque, which means you should determine exactly how you're going to ride most often. For example, two-up travel benefits from more torque at lower RPM levels, while chasing the checkered flag typically calls for high horsepower at high RPM levels. While we try to provide usage guidelines for all Screamin' Eagle' components, we can't test every possible combination. So please refer to the performance build-up dyno charts on the following pages, and remember to always consult with your Harley-Davidson dealer about performance-related issues.

CAMS AND COMPRESSION

Stock or moderate-lift "bolt-in" cams are most suited to stock-compression and smaller-displacement engines. Using a small-lift cam in high-compression applications typically puts a greater strain on your starting system. So make sure your starting system—which includes the battery, starter motor, cables and relays—is up to the task. In some extreme cases, such as with the installation of a high-compression "stroker" flywheel assembly, it may be necessary to install Screamin' Eagle manual compression releases in your cylinder heads so the engine turns over more easily on start-up.

VALVE SPRINGS

Changing cams may require the installation of new valve springs to accommodate a performance cam profile. When choosing a Performance Valve Spring Kit, consider both the RPM range and lift of the cams you're going to use—higher spring forces result in higher wear and friction, so you should never use a valve spring with a higher spring force rating than you need.

CLUTCH CONSIDERATIONS

Performance upgrades generally increase torque output, which can affect the clutch. When making performance enhancements, we recommend that you increase the torque capacity of your clutch with the installation of a Screamin' Eagle high-performance clutch spring or a complete clutch kit.

EFI AND PERFORMANCE

Electronic Fuel Injection (EFI) technology relies on an Electronic Control Module (ECM), a processor that determines the precise moment at which fuel is released into the cylinder to optimize engine performance. If any change is made to the engine and/or intake and exhaust systems of an EFI-equipped Harley-Davidson model, the ECM must be re-calibrated to maximize performance and prevent serious engine damage. Screamin' Eagle' offers not only numerous EFI calibrations for pre-determined street-legal and race-only component combinations, but also complete EFI Tuner Kits for '01-later Softail and '02-later Touring models. EFI calibration is a highly technical matter, so always consult your dealer when considering performance enhancements.

PERFORMANCE CAMS FOR TWIN CAM 88®-EQUIPPED MODELS, #25957-99A, page 463

JOE DUFFY Your motorcycles are works of art. What do you do to ensure your marketing communication efforts are held to the same standard?

TOM WATSON It all begins with the motorcycle — whether it is the styling of a new model, the design of a new accessory, or the creative development of the product literature or brand ads. This universal starting point provides clarity of purpose and consistency that is reflected in all of the work.

DUFFY Tell me how you first became involved with doing work for Harley-Davidson?

DANA ARNETT In 1985 I made a cold call on a gentleman by the name of Ken Schmidt. I found out he was working on helping the new Harley-Davidson management team put together a buy-out from AMF. Harley had been part of a very large conglomerate, which made everything from bowling balls to government missiles.

Harley was really the bastard stepchild in that the brand was suffering from a lot of negative publicity from what you might call the outlaw element. It was widely seen as the personality of the brand. So the 18 gentlemen who were in the management ranks of Harley decided that they would make an offer to buy the company back. They bought the company back and went public. Turns out that window of time between '84 and '87 was the right time to be calling on Harley. Besides, I have always had an interest in motorcycles and riding.

DUFFY Did you have a Harley at the time?

ARNETT No, actually, I could barely afford my rent. But you know, I grew up in Central Illinois. Instead of farms, it was full of motorcycle clubs surrounded by Harleys. Anything on two wheels around there was quite beautiful. I thought that there was a really interesting opportunity to get inside Harley somehow. So I showed up with my portfolio. I met a couple of people who were glad to see somebody who wanted to be part of what they were about — this journey they were about to take.

The first job we got was an information folder for the executives to use at meetings with investment bankers. And they liked it. The second thing we did was a campaign called "America's Fifty Best Roads," which allowed us to take a deeper step inside this enthusiast culture. It was maybe the only active, living, breathing, positive thing left at Harley. At that time, everything needed fixing, from the corporate culture to the motorcycles. The motorcycles had the lowest quality rating in the industry. The dealer network was poorly managed. And the brand had no traction whatsoever. The good that came out of it was that I was exposed to management. I was also exposed to the group in charge of turning the brand around. We were getting out there doing one-on-one experience marketing with the western-style riding enthusiast group.

DUFFY **Did they have an agency at the time?**

ARNETT Yeah, they were working with Carmichael on advertising. On the design and marketing side they really had no true agency of record. They had several small firms in

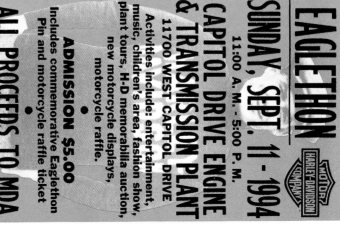

Milwaukee that were doing work for different departments. Carmichael was beginning to take hold of messaging at that time, so I must say we were really fortunate.

DUFFY So they had been there for a couple years?

ARNETT I think they had been there one or two years at the time. They were focused less on what you might call the brand turnaround and more on media placement and advertising. But there were some nice things being done. Nothing was really centrally coordinated, and I guess you might say the visual voice of Harley really hadn't materialized yet.

DUFFY So those early jobs started the ball rolling for positioning the brand?

ARNETT I think the thing that put it all together for us, and put it all together for Harley, was our first annual report. There was a three- or four-year window where we were just getting underneath the hood of the brand. But there was a whole bunch of mechanical things that needed to be fixed before Harley could even begin to think about coming together with the unified marketing message.

They had to reorganize some of the departments within the company. They had to take a serious look at their position on Wall Street. New management was slowly being hired and put into place. It wasn't until '89 that we were asked to do their annual report. I think the annual report was a breakthrough because we were asked to describe the whole company from a management perspective to what it's like to

Rider's Edge

Teach a person to ride, and you'll have a customer for life.

It's a simple equation. And it's the reason Rider's Edge® works. So maybe you should start putting the Rider's Edge New Rider Course to work for you. To learn how you can become a participating dealer, stop by the Rider's Edge booth in person, or call Michelle Rasmussen at 414.343.7031 or Tom Gillard at 414.343.4210. And make sure that you visit us online at www.ridersedge.com. Because Rider's Edge is not just an investment in your dealership. It's an investment in your future.

Rider's Edge

Your most loyal customer may not know how to ride yet.

Your future doesn't just depend on attracting new people to your dealership. It depends on attracting them to motorcycling. And Rider's Edge® can help you do both. To find out how to become a participating dealer, stop by the Rider's Edge booth in person, or call Michelle Rasmussen at 414.343.7031 or Tom Gillard at 414.343.4210. And make sure to visit us online at www.ridersedge.com. Because when you teach a person to ride, you make a customer for life.

be out there on the road or in a dealership or in the factory.

We were able to go out for about five months and meet people at rallies. We were everywhere — from Japan to Walkeroosa, Indiana — taking pictures, hearing stories, and beginning to really get the full-dimensional picture of Harley. And we were asked, of course, to package that picture. As we went through that process, we were getting a cultural message about how a brand can reinvent itself both as an organization and as a brand. So that was the neat little thread that we could run through all those verticals.

DUFFY **Was that the watershed moment?**

ARNETT We proved to ourselves and to the company that we had something special to build on. And it was exciting how the company's management was really supportive, interested, and attached to what we were doing.

DUFFY **Was there an individual visionary in the management group?**

ARNETT I would say Theo [Felsl], who had come over from Herman Miller. And I can't say enough about Rich Teerlink. Rich understood and invited everyone to play. He wanted us in the meetings, and he was out there at the rallies on his bike. So we became part of this family, as they call it at Harley. As we've grown as an agency, Harley has grown as well. Rich was a big part of the cultural and operational turnaround of the company. He was always searching for ways to stress its importance. On the marketing side, we were lucky enough to meet a couple people who had survived many years of frustration, complacency, and brand deterioration as well. They were ready to embrace an agency or two that could help them rebuild a brand.

DUFFY **Tom, tell us about the collaboration between your in-house marketing group and the outside design and advertising partners?**

WATSON As with all client-agency relationships, there is give and take in the creative process. Ultimately, the Harley-Davidson Marketing or Communications group is the final arbiter of brand values. However, we are fortunate to have a strong brand that provides everybody with an agreed-upon starting point and destination.

ARNETT Harley would call it "community building." They do have a very centralized marketing and communication function. But they also encourage people throughout the corpora-

tion to work with groups like VSA or Carmichael Lynch. So there's a neat little turbulent effect that results from us being involved and getting a chance to have our ideas heard deep within the company.

It wasn't as if we sat down in the beginning of the year and Harley said, "Okay, VSA, you are doing these 13 things. And Carmichael, you are doing these 20 things. It grew organically. We started with marketing and communications materials. Then we began doing events marketing. Then we were doing the parts and accessories business. We designed some of the lobby spaces, the annual report, and the dealership environmental graphics and signage program. Suddenly, when you started to line these things up, you could see this visual language begin to form.

What makes the work so powerful is that it's a reflection of what you see when you walk into a rally. You might see 750 different T-shirts with everything on them from "Ratfinks" to skull and crossbones. So we plastered our walls with this visual ensemble of the material we were seeing out there. We thought what we saw was a very blunt, irreverent perspective. It's deeply personal at times. So we tried to dump all the formalities and mannerisms of design. We were searching for something that had a real interesting honesty to it.

I think the projects that failed were the ones that went too far into an area of style. This is such an evangelistic customer base. The minute they see something that doesn't ring true to them, they are going to say something about it. So we are always walking that tightrope, which to me is great,

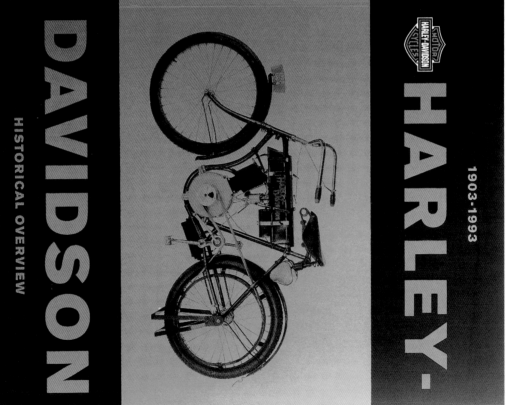

HARLEY-
1903-1993
DAVIDSON
HISTORICAL OVERVIEW

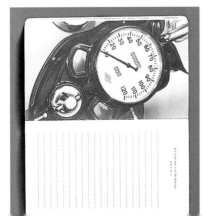

because it challenges us every day to do great work. We don't get complacent about a system of identity standards. We purposely don't get into that management trap.

DUFFY The restraint is fantastic because, as you have said, Harley is a quintessential honest American brand. You could take off in so many directions visually because of product, because of the audience, because of all the things that surround the brand. But I can see how it would be very easy to get off track.

ARNETT I'll tell you, you are right. I had a minor epiphany the first time I met Willie G. Davidson, who is the Director of Design and Vice President of Design and Styling at Harley. He's the great-great grandson of the founder. In fact, all of the family is involved in the corporation. Willie has been designing and directing design for the motorcycle core product for over 40 years. I remember being invited into his design studio, and he was doing lettering and color studies for the tank. I think it was for the A7 model. It was interesting. I said, "So you don't set any typography?" He said, "No, are you kidding? Every letter you see on a tank is hand drawn. Now, you'll see little subtle tweaks of a few familiar type faces, like Americana, but all of that is drawn." I was watching somebody get as uniquely engrossed in typography as he was in the styling of a fender or a belt cover. This guy had a complete holistic understanding of the machine. And ultimately, as they say at Harley, everything starts with the motorcycle and halos off of it. Again, this is another illustration of how design becomes powerful through many different channels of wisdom and style, and it's always been a nurtured aspect of Harley.

THE ONLY THING MORE UNIQUE THAN OUR

PRODUCTS
IS OUR CONSTANT DRIVE
TO IMPROVE THEM

DETERMINATION

HARLEY-DAVIDSON for 1930

PARTS & ACCESSORIES AREA

Even when the company was being poorly managed during the '60s and '70s, design was always a cornerstone of every-thing — from the design of their buildings to the bikes and the t-shirts. There's an embrace of design at Harley, and that's something you sometimes spend years trying to get clients to understand. I think we were successful because we understood this reality very early on.

WATSON Despite being a brand that has developed and evolved over the past 100 years, with various degrees of nuance and subtlety, at its core the Harley-Davidson brand is very straightforward. There are many ways to express what has been referred to as the Harley-Davidson "mystique," but there is great unanimity about the core brand attributes of freedom, authenticity, individualism and the spirit of adventure. These core brand attributes are well established, almost universally recognized, and act as a "brand compass" for all work.

DUFFY There are product designers, such as Willie G., who are very close to their work. And there are graphic designers, such as Dana, who are very close to their work. All these people have a vested interest in the brand. How do they know what the other is thinking?

WATSON The remarkable consistency of the Harley-Davidson creative and design work over the past years does not mean that it has not changed at all; it is reflective of the overall stra-tegic needs of the company. Yet, this process of change is as subtle as the Harley-Davidson brand itself. It is a process of evolution rather than revolution. Our ultimate goal is for

THE SHOVELHEAD ERA

anyone evaluating Harley-Davidson advertising, literature, or any brand communications from any department or any era to recognize the entire body of work as something as classic as the motorcycle itself.

DUFFY **Dana, do you ever collaborate with the product designers at Harley?**

ARNETT We've had meetings with them, but, you know, as in any automobile company or transportation company, there's a lockdown area so you can't get into the styling lab. But I've had a couple design sessions with Louie Ness and Willie G. on different special assignments. I was seeing them 10, 15 times a year at rallies. And we were sitting around either chewing the fat or passing the sketchbook, or Willie would say, "God, I saw that parts catalog you did. Beautiful shot of the Road King." Or we would create something for his department or another area of the company and it was almost, I hate to say it, like a brotherhood of motorcycle buddies, where you are almost high-fiving each other.

DUFFY **How about collaboration with Carmichael?**

ARNETT The only collaboration with Carmichael has been joint summit meetings where the marketing department tells us about the company's upcoming initiatives or plans. We never collaborated specifically on a project. But again, there's this real sense of family, and you know that they are not going to screw things up, and vice versa. I will say that there's a lot of interest on both sides in what we're doing; we are very careful to look at the language they are using and that we're

using so it all fits together. And then again, the marketing department gives each of us very specific direction so we're not messaging differently.

DUFFY Who is the primary governor of that messaging right now?

ARNETT Joanne Bishman, the Vice President of Advertising.

DUFFY I heard you say something once about being careful to allow the brand to be ahead of design. What did you mean by that?

ARNETT We are in a deeply personal business. It's hard for designers to step back and let the work be more important than they are. Our challenge here the last couple of years has been to take a brand that is so deeply infused with heritage, and find a way to inject it with youth and exuberance and speed. We're finding ways to elevate traditional elements with contemporary imagery, typography and language. But you never know — as quickly as you build a brand, you can also find yourself off the tracks.

That's our biggest challenge right now. Harley is bringing together the agencies, doing research, and having discussions to look at how to keep this brand alive and well for another 100 years. It's pretty safe to say that the demand for the product will continue to grow, but it's real noisy out there right now.

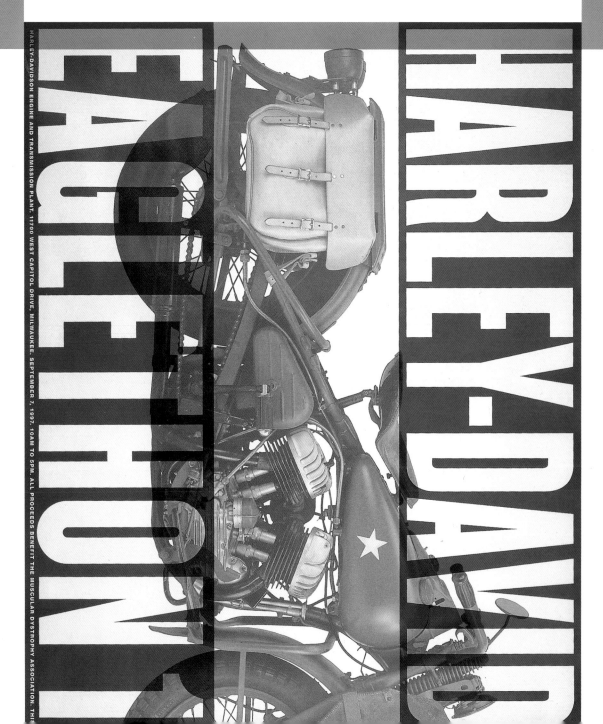

HARLEY-DAVID

EAGLETHON

HARLEY-DAVIDSON ENGINE AND TRANSMISSION PLANT, 11700 WEST CAPITOL DRIVE, MILWAUKEE. SEPTEMBER 7, 1997, 10AM TO 5PM. ALL PROCEEDS BENEFIT THE MUSCULAR DYSTROPHY ASSOCIATION. THIS

DUFFY Is there any work that you'll be producing within the next four or five months that you are excited about?

ARNETT The thing that captures the energy of what we do, which also tends to get the most recognition, is the annual report. We are in the midst of doing the 100-year annual report, which together with management, we decided would be a trilogy. So we're in book number two. Next year we will be doing book number three, so it will be a package set of these really beautiful documents. We have an appreciation for the tactile, the genuine quality of what we're working on.

The second thing we get excited about year after year is the parts and accessories marketing, which is, in essence, the packaging of customization. Next year I think the marketing effort will be a 900-page catalog. And it's everything cool that you put on your bike. Willie G. Davidson calls these things "rolling sculptures." You get a bike, and the first thing you do is customize it to be a reflection of yourself. So you'll see about 30 or 40 bikes in this catalog that were creations of the parts and accessories team, and we are giving people a look at what you can do with that palette. To me, that's where it gets real. You are playing around with the product and getting inspiration and influence from it. It makes me want to get out and ride today.

NONE MORE IMPORTANT THAN OUR CUSTOMERS' BODIES.

IDE IS DEDICATED TO VETERANS OF FOREIGN WARS.

BMW

CHALLENGE Precise and effective positioning for the BMW brand in North America attracted a crowd of me-too automotive brands, in effect watering down BMW's message.

SOLUTION Charged with the task of engaging a young, busy, cyber-savvy audience, Fallon Minneapolis began by starting over. Traditional advertising would no longer do the job.

RESULT The Hire, a revolutionary series of short films, collected enthusiasts and critical acclaim on its way to changing attitudes not only in prospective auto buyers, but also in Chief Marketing Officers, board rooms, and marketing media around the world.

JIM MCDOWELL former vice president, marketing [BMW OF NORTH AMERICA]

BRUCE BILDSTEN former creative director [FALLON WORLDWIDE]

KEVIN FLATT creative director, interactive [FALLON WORLDWIDE]

BMWFILMS.COM

JOE DUFFY Will you summarize the BMW brief for this project. What goals were outlined?

BRUCE BILDSTEN It began as a brief for a traditional advertising campaign, so we went to BMW with this traditional ad campaign. We looked at each other across the table and just said, "Geez," we can do more. And I asked Jim if we could go back and work on it again.

JIM MCDOWELL Then, we said to Fallon, if we allowed you to selectively ignore some of the things about BMW brand advertising that we have held sacred for a long time, what kind of idea would you come up with? We sent them a letter and that started a real stream of new thinking from the team in Minneapolis.

BILDSTEN In the letter they said, "We know we put a lot of rules on you." (And they do. Generally, there're a lot of rules to BMW advertising.) "We want you to take the cuffs off. And we want you to just come back and shock us with something. Really inspire us."

DUFFY **Talk about that letter. Why did you decide to write a letter?**

MCDOWELL If something is really important and we want to make certain that there is no miscommunication about it, we sit down and write a letter that we never intend to send.

DUFFY **But you did send the letter.**

MCDOWELL Yes. And I'm glad we did.

DUFFY **You suddenly had a whole new brief. A new objective. Maybe even new inspiration?**

BILDSTEN It was. We had been frustrated that we couldn't show what BMW could really do. We had been collecting clips of driving sequences from movies that we had always wanted to use in some way. One of them was a great chase scene in the movie "Ronin." We thought maybe we could do something to get people to want to visit us. Not like an ad, but like people want to watch these great scenes from great movies.

Once we had the idea to do films, we knew we wanted to promote them like real films. We would do trailers, so even our advertising would be like a Hollywood experience. And finally, we knew that it had to be an incredible interactive experience. That's what we presented to BMW.

DUFFY **What was the initial reaction when the idea was all laid out?**

BILDSTEN Ultimately, when we went back to BMW to present the idea, "Ronin" footage was one of the things we used. They made us replay it because it's so much fun to watch. It took us a half-hour to present the idea and 30 seconds for them to say yes. I mean, they instantly just loved it.

DUFFY **Talk about the meeting. You had written a letter and said let's take away the constraints. When Fallon came and presented the idea, what was your reaction and how did you feel?**

MCDOWELL The idea could have sounded to other groups like the Tower of Babel. It was a questionable idea added to a questionable idea, and how in the world could you propose

that? Yet, there it was on the table. We saw how different it was, and thought it would probably work. Because there were enough elements that we knew would fit with our psychographic, we were relatively confident. I would say that the most serious part of the discussion was what was the backup plan if we were wrong.

DUFFY **Did you know you could pull this off? Had you checked into it?**

BILDSTEN No. We just felt like we could. We thought, "What the heck?" After we presented the idea, we kind of went off in three camps. Kevin Flatt in the interactive team started

figuring out how they would execute the interactive. I think a lot of people didn't think that we would have the capability to do it all ourselves.

DUFFY **How about the client?**

BILDSTEN The client didn't think we could do it either. The client knew that we had done a great job with the Web site but thought that this would be overwhelming. Kevin sat down with them to say that this team could do it all. Another team went to Los Angeles and presented the idea to some huge-name Hollywood directors and production companies. And our account team worked on figuring out how to justify

the cost. They came up with a really interesting formula that stood up to incredible statistical scrutiny from BMW. In the end, the films cost no more than a downright traditional ad campaign all because they reversed the usual ratios for production. That's what is so brilliant about it.

DUFFY **Initially, did David Carter and Joe Sweet, the art director and writer, come up with the BMW Films idea and then come talk to you, Kevin? Or were you in on the initial brainstorming that led to the films' idea?**

KEVIN FLATT We were all on a creative retreat and I was sitting at a table with David and Joe while they were talking

with Mark Sitley, head of Fallon broadcast production. We started talking about how we could use the Web to deliver these films. We had to understand the limitations of the Web. A film on the Web couldn't be 60 minutes; it had to be shorter and smaller. That also led us to think about how we could take advantage of the Web in a different way. After a lot of other discussions, this led to us thinking about delivering a large file that you could download, taking advantage of your computer's speed.

DUFFY I'm assuming that you didn't move forward with an idea like this the same way you normally approach marketing ideas at BMW.

MCDOWELL Normally when we try to do something new, we get a community of people together to think it through from a variety of perspectives. Sometimes that results in us believing that we can do something far more adventurous than we ever would have dreamed of doing alone. But without a doubt something as dramatically different as this would never have survived that kind of process. What made our situation unique is that we have the best understanding of the psychographic of our potential customer of anyone in our competitive group. The films attracted so much attention because we did what everybody thought would be a great marketing campaign for 2003 in 2001.

DUFFY What was it like working with these kinds of directors versus working with traditional television commercial directors?

BILDSTEN We knew that we would have a much more hands-off approach with producing these films. We coached BMW on this. They totally agreed.

DUFFY Did you think it would be more difficult than it was to produce films where the cars got destroyed?

BILDSTEN Yes. Ultimately, none of the directors believed that the client would actually live up to their word. John Franken-

heimer at the end of shooting "Ambush" said to me, "I can't believe they let me do that. They really lived up to their word. It was wonderful."

DUFFY **How tough is scriptwriting for a film versus the typical 60-second spot or 30-second spot?**

BILDSTEN Well, even though they had virtually no screen-writing experience, Joe and David desperately wanted to write the scripts. They did that individually and as a team. We lined up some fairly big-name Hollywood screenwriters as well. We wrote a lot of scripts and they wrote a lot. Ultimately it ended up being more than 30 for the first batch of films. They were totally different stories. We wanted a variety of stories that would appeal to different people, even though each story would contain that same essential character. At least 20 were presented to BMW, who helped us further narrow it down. That's where they chose to exercise their control. They said that as long as we're comfortable with the stories, we know the directors will be able to interpret those stories in their own way. We'll give them a tremendous amount of freedom.

DUFFY **With BMW Films, obviously there's a BMW voice that comes from marketing communications, product, and BMW owner relationship standpoints. Then, there's the content of the films themselves, which is a critical component. How did you make sure your efforts on the interactive component combined with everything else to communicate in the same BMW voice?**

FLATT We worked closely with Bruce Bildsten, David Carter, Joe Sweet and Greg Hahn, another Fallon writer. Together we found what we felt was a proper voice and look. Based on our experience handling bmwusa.com sites, we kept in mind what would make sense in this environment for film viewing. So we weren't going to walk into your life and try to push a lease on you. We were going to appreciate that this is about entertainment and fun brought to you by a company that really appreciates high-performance vehicles. It's about taking things to a new level that connoisseurs can truly appreciate.

DUFFY **So there was a conscious effort to separate the**

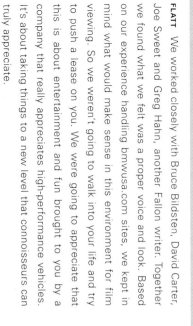

voice of the films from the voice that urges you to buy a BMW.

FLATT Absolutely. We wanted everybody to know that BMW was a part of it, but we didn't want them to feel like they were suddenly inside a dealership.

DUFFY **What things helped make that separation between church and state?**

FLATT The first season we had the areas of the site divided between machines and films, with the films being the first thing that was presented. After you saw the films, if you

wanted to explore the machines that the driver used, they were there. So there's always a user-controlled situation. If they didn't want to watch the films, they didn't have to. Oddly enough, results showed that people would check it all out. At least half, if not 75 percent, of the people were looking at the vehicles. We wanted to give them a taste, and if it was interesting, they could then go to the corporate site, the vehicle site, or the dealer site and dive in deeper.

DUFFY **Tell me how the different disciplines were brought together. How did you establish the teams and how did you get them to work together?**

BILDSTEN We were together on this thing from day one. Tom Riddle, a designer, worked closely with Kevin and his team, too. The design integration touched the advertising, touched the filmmakers and title design and ultimately the Web. It wasn't forced integration, it just happened.

FLATT As soon as we sold the idea, there was a lot of work to be done. David Carter would not have been able to focus on making these films as great as they were — guiding the thought process and sitting down to decide on five posters and 20 print ads — if he were still jumping around New York and Hollywood and everywhere else. Tom Riddle was able to take what David had already started and make it great film

design. I kept him in tight with our Web designers to help bridge the overall assignment.

DUFFY **So they were shooting the films before you figured out the final technology solution?**

FLATT At one point we had to make a decision that my team would focus on the theater while Bruce and his team and the broadcast department focused on the films. We were building the theater as they were making the films.

DUFFY **Let's talk results. How did your expectations going in compare to the actual results?**

MCDOWELL We assumed there would be a ramp-up curve and then a relatively stable volume of people watching the films over time. We did not properly anticipate how cumulative the effect would be. We were delighted that people came to see the first film. The combination of the first and second films had a much bigger volume than expected. When the third film came out, there was no question we were going to meet our two million target. The question was: Is this going to keep increasing because if it is, we don't have anywhere near enough servers? In that first season, we ended up getting six and a half times as many people as had been our objective.

BILDSTEN It's always difficult to tie direct sales to something like this. We did a tremendous amount of pre- and post-research. BMW is very smart about results, so we didn't go into this blind and just try to guess afterwards. There were a lot of verbatims from people who said, "Gee, I had a Lexus and an Audi on my shopping list and I saw the films and I thought I would look like a wimp buying one of those cars. I had to buy the BMW." There were some dramatic shifts in attitude about BMWs: BMW being fun to drive; BMW being for me; BMW being for young people; even, BMW is safe.

DUFFY If someone sees a film that features the X5, is there a way to track that they have gone from the film site to the car site, looked at the X5, and then actually followed through on the purchase?

FLATT With all the films we set up a connection between the

film and the featured vehicle. The viewer can learn a little bit about the vehicle attributes and link to bmwusa.com from there. Once on the bmwusa site, they can link to a dealer locator to set up a test-drive with the dealer. Based on the increased traffic, which we tracked throughout that process, it worked quite well.

DUFFY These films have made an impact beyond North America.

FLATT Before we even had the first film launched, we had people signing up to receive updates. And even though this was truly a North American push, we were getting people from Germany and other parts of the world. The night we uploaded the first film, we had about 60 people from outside the states. We thought it was a mistake, so we ran the test

again and we got 230 some-odd people. The number just kept growing. From the very get-go, we had international interest.

DUFFY What about all the buzz, all the PR, all the things over and above what you signed up for that got the brand out there?

BILDSTEN Well, first of all it was really beneficial to BMW. I think they ended up having something like 25 billion dollars worth of free exposure. Stories about these films have run in 1,800 media outlets.

DUFFY Does this open the door for convincing clients that they should do more than just a traditional TV spot?

BILDSTEN The future is in media that rewards a viewer for their time as opposed to imposing on them.

DUFFY Do you see other possibilities for this type of approach to brands?

FLATT Absolutely. I'll tell you this, though. BMW Films is unique in that it's a very brave and courageous client with an incredible product. That will lend itself to this kind of thing, but that may not always be the perfect formula for every brand out there.

DUFFY What was the biggest lesson learned?

BILDSTEN I'll be honest with you, when we actually sold this thing, there was a certain amount of fear and dread. Because

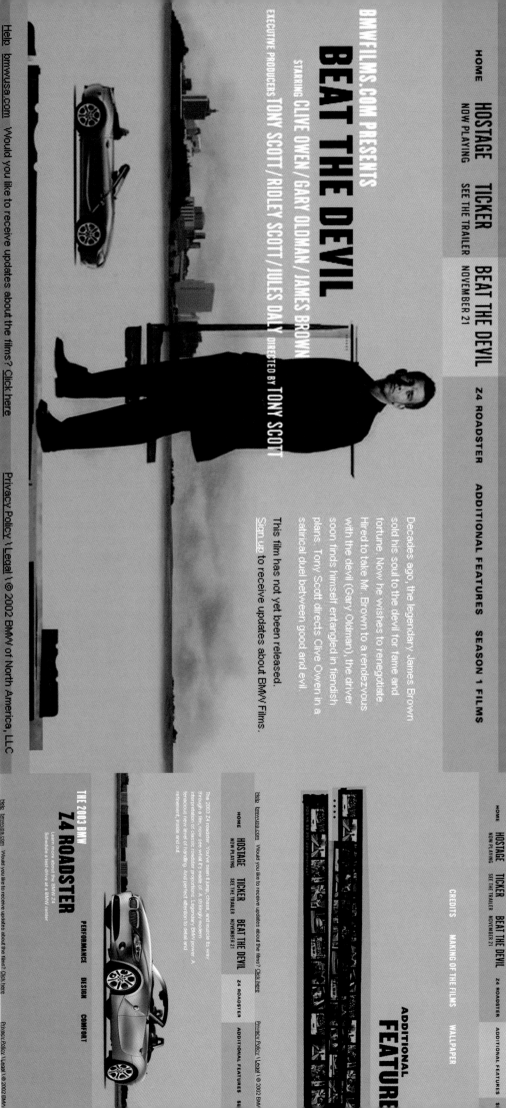

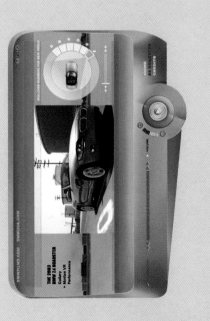

I knew it was going to be a tremendous amount of work. And it was — over a hundred people were involved in this at Fallon. It was all night and all day. I mean, there were some people who couldn't bear to work on the second batch.

DUFFY Obviously, you've raised the bar. This has broken new ground. It's the talk of advertising the world over. For BMW specifically, where's the next level? Where do you go from here?

BILDSTEN There's a tremendous amount of equity in "The Hire." There's a lot of equity in the driver, played by Clive Owen. And it may be a new batch of films. But it may be something different as well. Studios have approached us

— television networks — wanting to turn it into movies and television series. BMW is being very careful.

DUFFY Is this something that could be an ongoing program?

MCDOWELL Even though we have debuted all the films, a lot of people watch them every week. What we discovered from the first round is that you can stop releasing and promoting films and people will still come day in and day out nearly forever. There are a lot of opportunities. But it's not as though we immediately want to make a decision. We want to see how long the response continues for these films.

CITI

CHALLENGE To rebrand the world's largest bank and redefine the financial services partner of the future.

SOLUTION Do everything possible to be unbank-like so that we can attract great marketing partners and real customers with everyday financial needs throughout their many life phases.

RESULT New branding and new brand language that speaks to real people. Amazingly, this solution has maintained its effectiveness and flexibility, allowing the voice to remain resonant through significant economic upheavals, including 9/11, the fall of many corporate executive ranks, and the subsequent U.S. stock market crash and resulting depressed world economy.

ANNE MACDONALD managing director of global marketing [CITIGROUP]

PAULA SCHER partner [PENTAGRAM DESIGN]

DAVID LUBARS former president worldwide/executive creative director [FALLON WORLDWIDE]

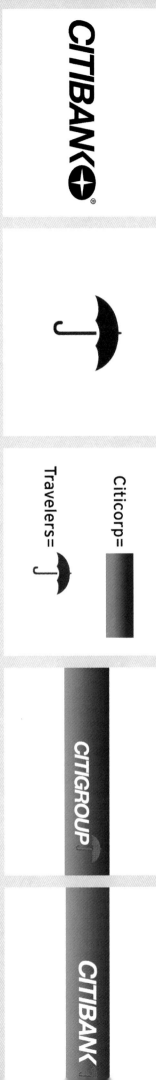

JOE DUFFY How did the process begin?

ANNE MACDONALD We had just undergone the merger of Citibank and Traveler's Group. It doubled the size of the bank, making us the biggest in the world. And we had to find a path to become one company. To be honest, we didn't know what the right model was. We had never done this before. But we were excited by the opportunity.

One of the first things I did was call Susan Avarde, Director of Global Branding. She came to my office and we shut the door. We started talking and thinking about what this could be. What it should be. Who should we work with? Neither of us had done something like this so big before. Frankly, there really aren't many opportunities like this that present themselves in one's career — the biggest bank in the world. We knew of Pentagram's work, so we picked up the phone and called them.

DUFFY When you called Pentagram, what did you say? How did you present the opportunity?

MACDONALD Well, we knew we had a sale to make. We knew

we needed to convince them that they would be able to do great work for a big, bad organization — especially a bank. So we thought a little bit about what might make them believe us. We really wanted them to take us seriously.

PAULA SCHER Citibank said they needed a new logo in four weeks because they needed to announce the merger to the press. We laughed because we knew there was no way that a global brand like that would be able to decide on a new logo in four weeks. So we went into this thing with a sense of humor. We had no expectations. It was fun. I have to say it was quite terrific because we were going about this project, and we didn't believe it was really going to happen. But at the same time it was very serious. It's just that it wasn't done in the buttoned-down way that many people would have expected with such a huge organization like Citi.

But it was the right work. The instincts in the thinking were right. I'm sure it's the most reproduced trademark I'll ever do in my life.

MACDONALD The assignment was to figure out a name for this new bank and to design the logo that the bank would

carry. We knew we needed to make the brand much more accessible. Our brief for everything we were doing — developing the brand, communications, products and the overall experience — was to be "refreshingly unbank -like."

We showed up at the Pentagram offices in New York. I think we surprised them because it was just two of us to brief them on this huge project. And they surprised us as well. Michael Beirut (a partner at Pentagram) was actually the one who greeted us at the door. We met with Michael and Paula. Right away, we hit it off.

SCHER The truth is, we had things mostly figured out after that very first meeting.

DUFFY Does that happen very often with your work?

SCHER My best work is often my first idea.

DAVID LUBARS It's true. The initial inspiration is usually the best. It's so clear. It's more than professional, it feels like it comes from somewhere magical.

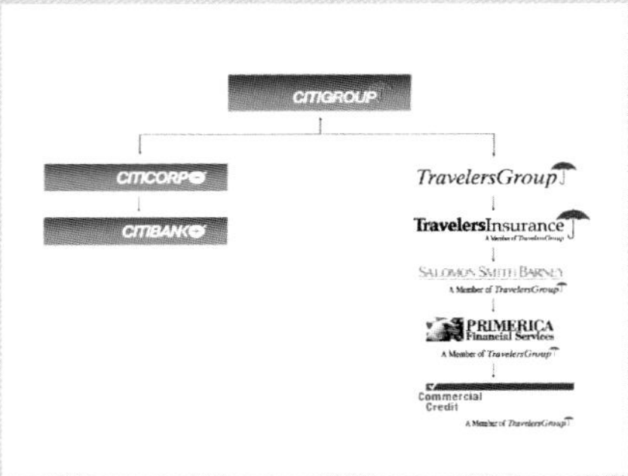

citi CITI citi CITI citi
(citi) (citi) **CITI** citi **citi**
Citi CITI citi citi

These are all Blue Waves

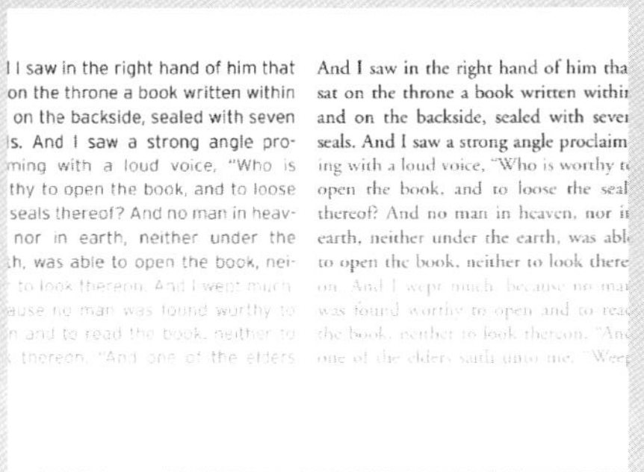

COKE
NIKE
SONY
C I T I

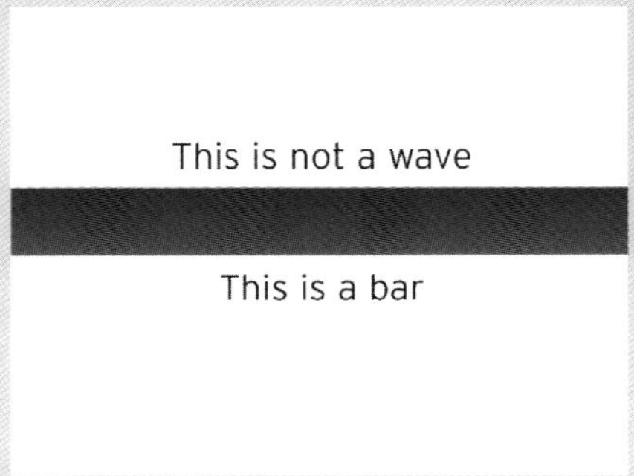

This is not a wave

This is a bar

citi

I saw in the right hand of him that And I saw in the right hand of him that
on the throne a book written within sat on the throne a book written within
on the backside, sealed with seven and on the backside, sealed with seven
ls. And I saw a strong angle pro- seals. And I saw a strong angle proclaim
ming with a loud voice. "Who is ing with a loud voice. "Who is worthy to
thy to open the book, and to loose open the book, and to loose the seal
seals thereof? And no man in heav- thereof? And no man in heaven, nor in
nor in earth, neither under the earth, neither under the earth, was able
h was able to open the book, nei- to open the book, neither to look there-
to look thereon. And I wept much on. And I wept much, because no man
ause no man was found worthy to was found worthy to open and to read
and to read the book, neither to the book, neither to look thereon. "And
the book, neither to look there- one of the elders saith unto me, "Weep

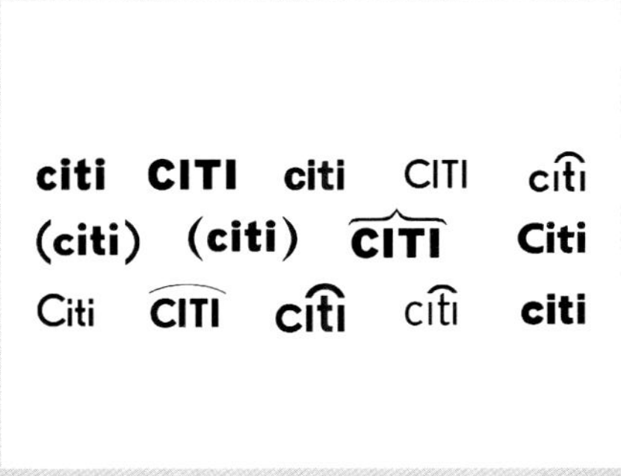

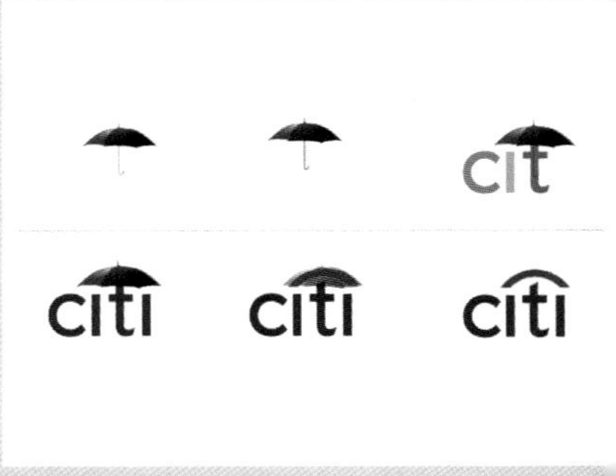

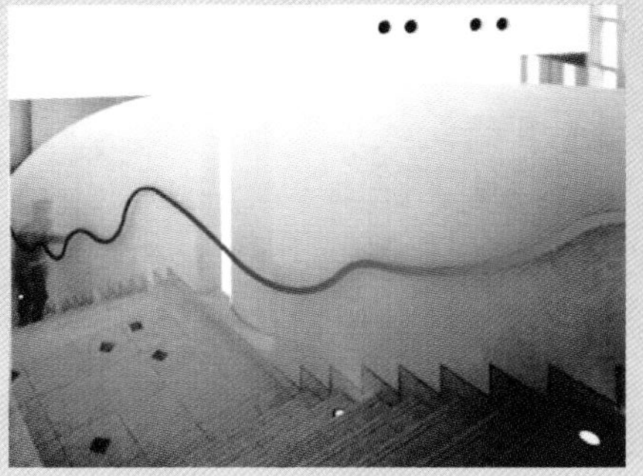

SCHER But it can be a problem, too, because it's hard to sell your first idea. People don't think you've done the necessary exploration. That's the problem with design. It doesn't happen like that. It's intuitive. It's a process that's not describable. It's an amalgamation of the last 17 movies you've seen, every-thing you know about European art, and what Citibank has told you about their brand. It's a spontaneous act. It doesn't have to do with appropriate methodologies.

DUFFY **Did the client know it was your first idea?**

SCHER No, not at the time, but they do now. We went back and looked at all the other possible ways we might do things. We needed to prove that we really did have the right solution and that there wasn't a better answer and that it hadn't been printed in the newspapers after the first four weeks.

What we did in those first four weeks was figure out the strategy that would eventually get the organization to buy the name Citi in its shortened form. It took much longer than that to actually make the sale. Interestingly enough, the logo itself had nothing to do with the strategy behind getting everyone to agree to the logo. A logo is a logo. It didn't take very long to figure out what we had to do with it. But it took

two years after we did figure it out to get the organization to commit to it. That's the really difficult stuff.

I have to give Susan and Anne and the rest of the client team all the credit in the world. They persevered with this thing. They made it happen. Anytime you see anything really good happen, you know there are some terrific clients doing it.

DUFFY **Tell us more about your initial thinking and what you figured out at that first meeting.**

SCHER There were a couple of things we were absolutely clear about. One of them was that we thought Citibank had to be shortened to Citi. Then I made a sketch on a napkin. I figured that lowercase "t" could be the handle of an umbrella if you put an arch on the top. That was essentially it. "Citi" made the bank more approachable, simpler. The umbrella brought the whole organization and these two entities together.

MACDONALD This approachability issue was critical because we were on a mission to become the bank of the future. New rulings had recently allowed us to be more than just a traditional bank, to provide insurance services as well. This allowed us to help our customers with all their financial

Diversify, divers

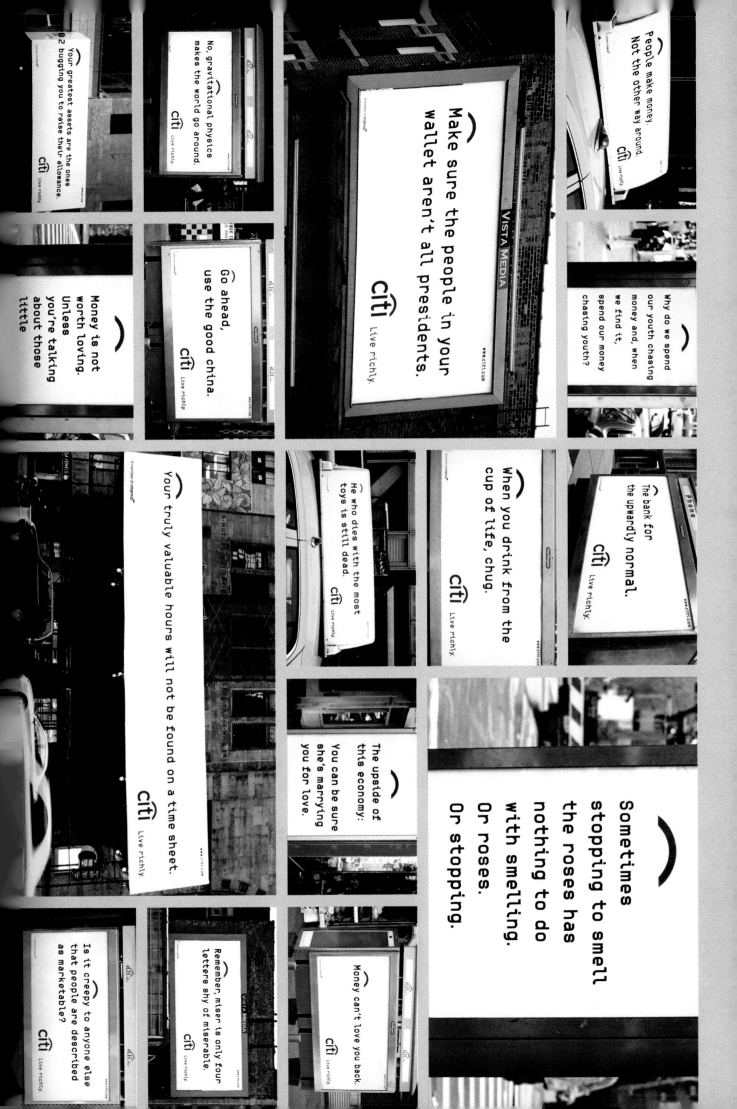

People make money.
Not the other way around.
citi Live richly.

Your greatest assets are the ones
@ 2 bugging you to raise their allowance.
citi Live richly.

No, gravitational physics
makes the world go around.
citi Live richly.

Make sure the people in your
wallet aren't all presidents.
VISTA MEDIA
citi Live richly.
www.citi.com

Why do we spend
our youth chasing
money and, when
we find it,
spend our money
chasing youth?
citi Live richly.

Money is not
worth loving.
Unless
you're talking
about those
little

Go ahead,
use the good china.
citi Live richly.

The bank for
the upwardly normal.
citi Live richly.
www.citi.com

When you drink from the
cup of life, chug.
citi Live richly.
www.citi.com

He who dies with the most
toys is still dead.
citi Live richly.

Your truly valuable hours will not be found on a time sheet.
A member of citigroup
SAVINGS
citi Live richly.
www.citi.com

The upside of
this economy:
You can be sure
she's marrying
you for love.

Sometimes
stopping to smell
the roses has
nothing to do
with smelling.
Or roses.
Or stopping.

Is it creepy to anyone else
that people are described
as marketable?
citi Live richly.
www.citi.com

Remember, miser is only four
letters shy of miserable.
VISTA MEDIA
citi Live richly.

Money can't love you back.
citi Live richly.

needs — banking, investments, insurance. It was the beginning of the future of banking.

SCHER And if you're a mega-institution — the biggest bank in the world — you need to be thinking about who your billionth customer might be, when he or she might walk into the bank for the first time, and what your bank stands for in 2012. That's what you need to think about when you design the identity.

We had a photograph of an 11-year-old girl. We made the case that she didn't care about whether or not Citibank's blue wave or Traveler's umbrella was a part of the new identity. That doesn't mean anything to her. What she's going to understand and care about is big, simple, overarching brands that live in her world. Like Coke and Nike and Microsoft — brands that are recognizable symbols with simple names.

She's not going to understand the difference among Citicorp, Citigroup, and Citibank. None of that will make sense to her. So we pictured her in the midst of all these brands and put a simplified Citi logo in there, and there became this incredible prevailing logic for it. Because you saw this big idea, this big bank, and this big brand that was simple enough, it was understandable over time.

DUFFY **Sounds like a great presentation. But you said it took two years to finally sell the logo. Tell us more about that.**

SCHER From my previous 30 years of experience in working with these processes and personalities, I've learned that identity development is not only intuitive on the client side, but highly emotional. It has to do with being able to embrace something as your badge. Once that happens, they have personal ownership. You need to let that happen. The organization needs to have ownership.

Beyond that, we knew there were two things that would make the logo happen from a functional perspective. We knew that as soon as the advertising hit the street, the logo would be adopted. The second and biggest thing was to get it on the bankcard. The minute it's on a debit card, it's a done deal.

Your current balance
should have nothing to
do with how much money
is in your account.

There's too much
good stuff

out there to
spend your time
focusing on
dollars and cents.

That's why
we offer tools
like free financial
check-ups.

And My Citi,
which keeps
all your
online accounts,
from banking
to airline miles,
in one place.

Because time
shouldn't always be

just about money.

Visit us at citi.com.

aol keyword citi   citi.com

citi
Live richly.

Save money.
Hoard friends.

You ordered a ten-speed bike.
And got ten speed-bikes.
Hello, Citi.

DUFFY **What was the relationship between the various partners and how did the process work?**

MACDONALD We work really hard on our side to be sure that our team has expertise in what they're doing and understands with whom they're working. We try to limit the number of contacts our agency partners have and the chain they have to go through. This allows us to engage with extremely talented people and to protect ourselves from ourselves. At the end of the day, we have a small team that respects collaboration and the collective IQ. It's really no more formal than that.

SCHER The only real caveat we made was to put the logo on everything and make it really clear. Put it everywhere.

LUBARS It worked because their goals were our goals. We took cues from the design because it was a great place to start. We knew we all needed to make the bank more accessible and more human. The last thing the world needs is another bank pointing its finger at you, saying, "Save for college; put some money away; do this and use these products."

We wanted to position Citi as an empathetic person sitting across the table from you, talking about stuff that matters. That's really how all the design and the film and the words were put together — white space, simple and clean, conversational. We're not talking to people who objectify money. We're talking about a healthy approach to money and a healthy approach to life. And Citi is the bank that understands

that. It's an authentic need, and that insight drove our work.

DUFFY **Where does it go from here?**

MACDONALD I think about that a lot. I know we need to save ourselves from becoming bored with something before the consumer does or before it's really old. I think that's a bad habit for many of us inside the business. We need to manage the evolution and stay attuned to the brand and the culture. I hope this can last for 25 or 30 years. It should. Brands, like people, need to build relationships, to elicit emotions, engage in dialogue, have a personality, a voice and a language. We still have a lot to do to bring all our efforts in line with this new brand position, to deliver the experience. That's what we're working on now.

NIKE

CHALLENGE One brand demanding excellence at every point. Thousands of products across myriad categories. The need to stay fresh in hundreds of countries, with millions of individual athletes in every sport imaginable. And do it all while balancing the varied reputations of fashion, function, and cultural buzz.

SOLUTION Use the brand culture as the central element. Speak passionately from the heart. Find inspiration in cultural and brand flexibility.

RESULT A touchpoint for debate and inspiration around the world in product, sport, business, accomplishment, and communications. Masterfully balance the distance between being always fresh, yet always Nike.

ROB DE FLORIO former director of U.S. global advertising [NIKE]
DAN WIEDEN president [WIEDEN+KENNEDY]
JOHN JAY creative director [WIEDEN+KENNEDY TOKYO]

tag play

JOE DUFFY **The concept for this book centered around the idea of one voice. Do you want to begin there?**

DAN WIEDEN The idea of one voice is a good place to start. I think one voice is an interesting proposition. There's something that feels really necessary about it today, especially with all the acquisitions going on in the business world. Suddenly overnight, brands find themselves being surrendered to larger brands. In many cases, there's not a lot of culture that holds these brands together; so creating a voice becomes a critical thing, but it's difficult to pull off. On the other hand, I think that sometimes the drive for unity can become so phony that nobody is talking honestly. And that worries me, because to be truly effective, we all need to speak from our hearts.

tag play

DUFFY **What I call "one voice" may be better described as a brand language that can speak in many voices in order to keep it interesting and refreshing.**

WIEDEN You're right. At the end of the day, I think what we are really trying to do is create an open feeling so that people can hear the brand. Who is talking and why is it talking to me? Does it have anything worth listening to? Most marketing, on the other hand, is based on a manipulative formula that selfishly asks, what do I want to tell these people and what do I want these people to do? That approach degrades the validity of the communication. Many of Nike's strongest campaigns are a product of understanding these subtle differences. I think when creative people internalize the brand and business issues and come up with something very personal; then, the idea becomes universal.

Air Jordan from Nike.

DUFFY Yes, I agree. Can you tell us more about your experiences in developing a brand language for Nike — one that has the range to speak to multiple audiences in multiple places, yet be the voice of a universal brand?

WIEDEN What truly is one of the most fascinating things about the Nike brand is that it speaks to so many distinctly different audiences. In the classical sense anyway, the voice that would speak to a young kid playing basketball at Rutger's Park is entirely different from the voice that would speak to a kid playing tennis in the Hamptons, or one playing football in Brazil, for that matter. If you try to unify that voice in the classic way, you end up watering it down to where it's common and uninteresting. It becomes no more than a

"voice of marketing," and it reaches only the lowest common denominator.

Instead, we speak to distinctly different audiences so that the athlete says, "Wow, those people understand me; they understand my sport in a way no one else does," and we make a connection that way. The dangerous thing about that is, if the client doesn't have a culture, a very distinct culture, that fragmented voice becomes totally schizophrenic.

It's a really interesting dilemma. I think at some point one voice can become the voice of a monopolistic person you really don't care about. So if things are too neatly tied up and orchestrated, there's the danger of ringing false. That's

why I believe the Nike "Just Do It" campaign has run so long. It's not specific. It's not talking about Nike per se, it's talking about professional athletes and fitness folks. It even extends beyond them. Within the "Just Do It" message, we are allowed many different voices that are true to that single observation and its many motivating forces.

ROB DE FLORIO On this issue of a brand language, we have a couple of basic philosophies at Nike that I continue to hammer home daily. One of them is exactly what Dan's talking about: Consistency doesn't mean sameness.

To me, effective consistency is emotional consistency. It's an understanding of what and how your brand makes the

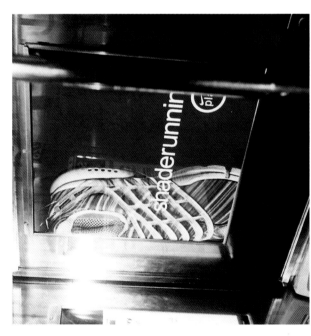

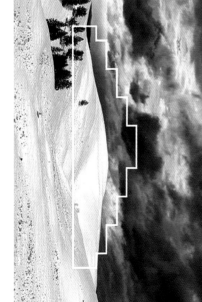

consumer feel. As a matter of fact, if you really know what your brand is about, and the people who work on the brand really know, whether they are in Shanghai or in Brussels, one thing everyone shares is the true meaning of the brand. This knowledge actually liberates everyone, encouraging them to be experimental and try different things. Still, it comes from the same core. Nike spends a lot of time and money doing pretty elaborate internal presentations for sales meetings, internal education, and new employees to drive home who we are and what we stand for and what we're passionate about. There are times I'm even frustrated with how much we spend internally. I start thinking we should focus our energy outside because that's where the attraction really is in the marketplace. But then I remind myself that it's really important that everyone knows the true meaning of the brand.

The other basic philosophy is integration. Integration is the

thing. Integration doesn't mean sameness, either. Integration starts at strategy. I believe consistency is emotional. I believe integration is strategic. I think too often the answer to both is sameness. And it's absolutely not true. If you are strategically integrated and know how five different pieces are going to work toward the same goal, then the pieces don't have to look like each other. I give this speech internally in our marketing division meetings on every project at least once a month. We need to constantly remind ourselves.

DUFFY I know from my experience that it's not always easy to deliver this consistency nor work in a truly integrated way. So many times the intentions are there, but it falls down in the realities of the day to day. The process of integrating multiple teams is a common struggle for people in our business. For Nike the teams range from your product designers and graphic designers to design

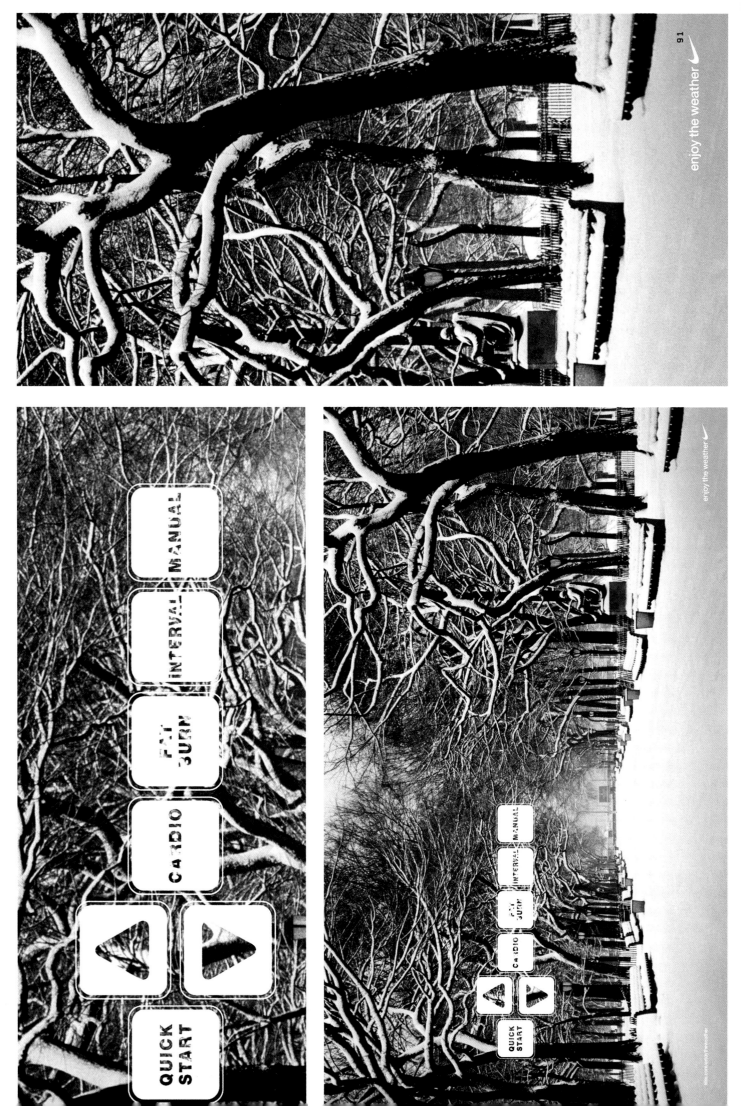

enjoy the weather ✓

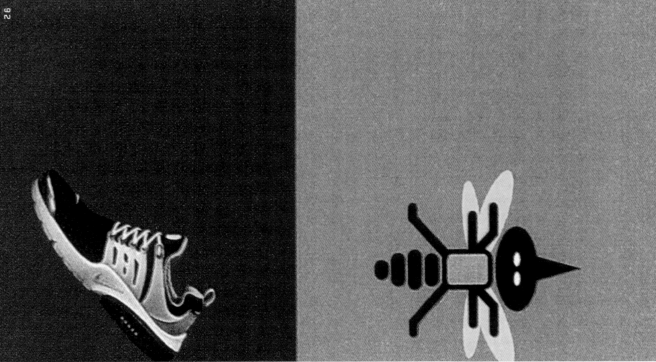

firms and ad agencies. How do you coordinate the integration of these teams?

DE FLORIO On the client side of the table, we set up a system where we have marketing communication managers and directors who are assigned to particular projects or products or sports categories. Their job is to look across all teams and media to make sure we are firing on all cylinders. At the same time, we have functional expertise in all of those areas. We have the best of the best in the PR group, the sports marketing group, the advertising group, our entertainment marketing groups, and in our product design group.

This creates a constant and healthy tension. We have a pretty high level of opinionated, successful, accomplished people in each area.

Someone asked me once, "When does it get easier?" I say, "It never gets easier." The point is, it has to be hard. You have to have that healthy tension. The combination of having good marketing people who understand what you want to get done, combined with functional expertise, is a tension-filled winning recipe. If you take the easy road, you won't reach the highest level.

DUFFY How and when do you integrate the people respon-

sible for product, in-store and packaging design with the team at Wieden? Or, is the work completed in-house and then shared with external partners?

DE FLORIO I've established this triad briefing process that works well. The ad team, the digital team and the in-house image design team get briefed on the project at the same time. The reason for doing that is twofold. One, a good idea can come from anywhere. If all the teams are in the room together and they know each other a little bit more and there's a sense of mutual respect, then there's less of a competitive turf thing.

Two, we reinforce that everyone's operating from the same strategy. If we all decide that execution doesn't have to be exactly the same because we're strategically in the right place, each team can feel comfortable adding its touch.

That said, the process is not easy. For example, the product design folks are still cycled a little bit ahead of everyone else because there is so much R&D tied directly to product design. Fortunately, we're getting the R&D folks more involved now.

JOHN JAY Collaboration is absolutely critical, because while great product design may not need great advertising, advertising always needs great product design.

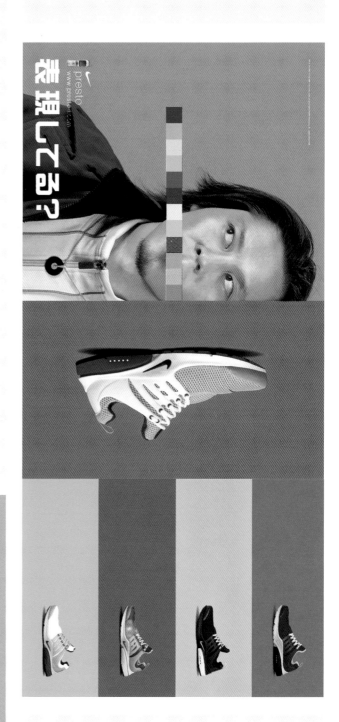

DE FLORIO I just think the only thing you can do in a situation with all this talent is maintain an environment where the creativity can thrive. That is easier said than done when you think about what it really takes for ideas to thrive. How do you avoid the things that can really kill them? Too much process kills things. Too little process leaves you nowhere, throwing stuff against the wall. The challenge is to find a balance between process and experimentation.

If you don't encourage people to engage, you're not going to get anywhere. You're just going to get more products of the same minds over and over again.

For example, something popped across my screen recently. One of our writers sent a message to one of our Group Ad

Directors. He wrote, "I was watching TV last night and the guys were talking about the World Cup and how irrelevant it is in this country. Anyway, it pissed me off and made me think maybe we need to wake these people up a little bit. So I wrote this ad." I love that. He was listening, he got pissed off, and that made him want to wake these people up. No brief, nothing. This writer decided to do something.

We've produced quite a few things that our creatives just popped off out of nowhere because they got irritated or touched by something. When we get the extreme emotions on either end of the process, we get the best work.

DUFFY Dan, John, are there traits that you look for in deciding who should work on Nike at your shop?

WIEDEN The kinds of people who work on this account and have over the last 20 years is so varied. Sometimes I put somebody on the account and they stretch in a really terrific way and they bring something new to the voice that is still relevant. They bring to life a side of the brand personality that you haven't seen before, and that's what keeps the work fresh.

DUFFY Do you have designers who will work on certain campaigns with an art director/writer team, or do you have art directors who wear both hats?

WIEDEN We don't really separate it in a traditional way. Designers sometimes do art direction, and art directors sometimes do design.

君 し か で き な い プ レ イ を し よ う

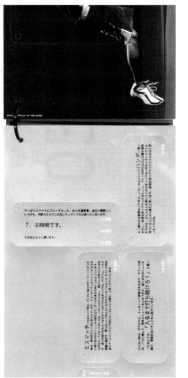

DUFFY What's your definition of creative direction?

JAY Not to be overbearing, as if you are doing the work yourself. Not to be underwhelming in influence, as if you are trying to be every creative's best friend. To put all of your cultural and professional life experiences to work. To be a great listener. To inspire. To put all ego aside and make those around you better. To demand and fight for great work.

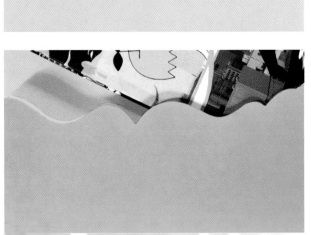

JAY We really try not to speak in terms of below or above the line, but rather just in ideas. They are of equal value and shouldn't be separated. There should be no hierarchy or status associated with who is more important — the designer or the art director. Those titles are industry creations.

DUFFY **Is there a set process for approvals? Or does final say shift from one manager to the next based on the most important issue at hand?**

JAY No formulas allowed.

DE FLORIO It's always different. The decision process has

to defer to the most important objective on that particular project. There has to be compromise. But you can't compromise to the point of making something less than it is supposed to be. Instead of compromising your standards, you find a way to work together. We do have a small consensus decision process. I emphasize the word "small" because when you get too broad, you either get no decision or a very watered-down one. Again, it comes down to a combination of marketing strategy and functional expertise.

DUFFY **As a designer who's part of an advertising group, occasionally it's my job to extend the big idea from a TV spot to work in-store or on the Web. It can be a difficult**

proposition if the idea isn't pliable enough. Do you do anything to avoid that kind of situation?

WIEDEN Normally we don't worry about that too much. I think if a spot works, generally there's a theme line or something that can hold all the work together. If not, the big blockbuster television idea probably isn't really doing its job.

DUFFY There has been so much good work done for this brand. Is there any one thing about this client or the brand that enables your teams to keep the thinking fresh

and do great work? Do you have greater creative liberty or get better briefs?

WIEDEN There's no set process. That's the key to this. What really makes it work is a client who, at the end of the day, is both extraordinarily curious and very courageous. We can go off-brief and we don't have to think up wild excuses as to why we are off-brief. The issue becomes the idea. Is it working? Does it work as hard as it could? It's a very flexible process. Going into the process with preconceptions that you have to live with would be like Columbus saying, "No, this has to

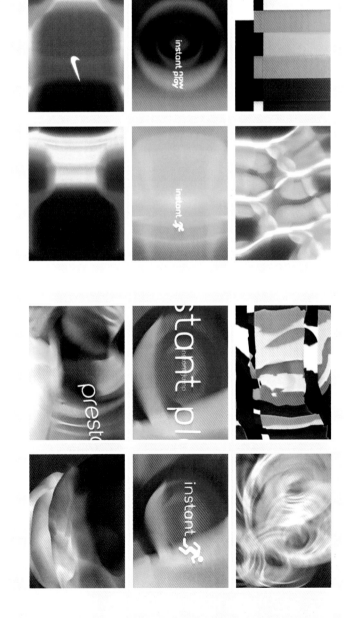

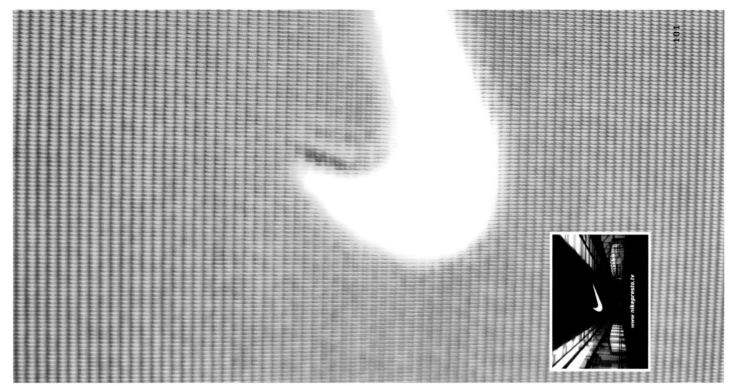

be India because that's what it says here, and that's what I set out to find." Sometimes we just find different things that work far better.

JAY I'd say it's all about trust — a trust you need to earn. Nike has built a culture of high expectations and excellence in all aspects of their business. One person, one product, one division at a time. Because the core of Nike is the athlete, there is a trust of personal intuition. Thus, the best at Nike still listen and act upon their hearts as well as their heads. I'd say they are tougher than most clients because of their expecta-

tions for creative excellence from the opening bell. And they know what is good and what isn't. That comes from both the DNA and the training.

They don't call it a "campus" for nothing.

MINI

CHALLENGE With a significant track record abroad and an extremely successful family member in the states (BMW), MINI set out to create a new car culture in the U.S. with zero awareness of the brand name.

SOLUTION Be true to the brand identity, but reinterpret it for its new market. Create a new culture. Don't rely on the traditional means of communications; namely, television and print advertising.

RESULT Sales goals were accomplished through nontraditional car marketing norms. The new motoring culture is flourishing.

KERRI MARTIN former director of marketing [MINI USA]

ALEX BOGUSKY creative director [CRISPIN PORTER + BOGUSKY]

LET'S MOTOR.™

MINI COOPER

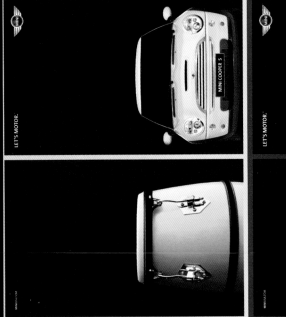

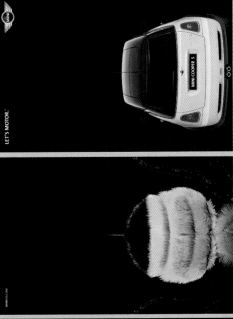

LET'S MOTOR.™ MINI COOPER S

LET'S MOTOR.™ MINI COOPER

LET'S MOTOR.™ MINI COOPER S

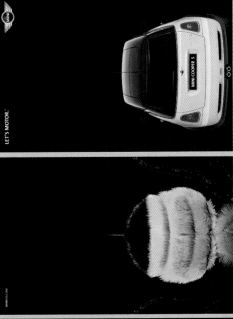

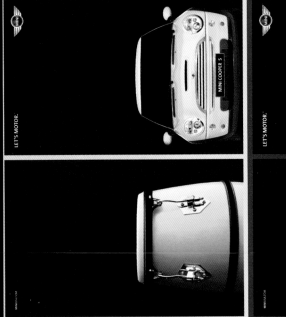

JOE DUFFY Congratulations on a simply marvelous campaign. Everyone I know admires it and is jealous of it. The more I see it the more I realize it epitomizes what we're trying to showcase: brand-building campaigns that utilize a full range of communications with one voice to make a powerful brand. And, you guys have been so successful at that. Tell us how this whole program got started — how it was presented to you from the client and what the brief was.

ALEX BOGUSKY It started in a pitch. While MINI was launched as a global brand, the situations in the U.K. and the U.S. were such that they realized there was a need for some market-specific thinking.

One of the first things that we found most interesting was from the RFP. In it, they referred to what they were looking for, not as an agency, but as a brand advocacy partner. And we thought, "Well that's really interesting. They're not asking for an agency."

We call ourselves an agency, but we definitely struggle with it all the time. The current definition suggests that you are going to do some TV commercials and print ads. Our point of view is that it's our job to make our clients or their products or their ideas famous, and we will use whatever means possible to do it.

Think about it: People and things become famous in our culture all the time. And they rarely use advertising to get

there. That's really the basis of our approach. So, one of the first things we did was to go back to the people at MINI and ask them, "Do you really mean it? And what does it really mean?" And that is where the chemistry really started.

KERRI MARTIN The brief presented a three-fold challenge: 1) Introduce an entirely new brand into the automotive market, (2) Launch two new models — the MINI Cooper and the MINI Cooper S, and (3) Create an entirely new segment within the category. And, of course, we had to do it all with limited resources. With that, our challenge to the finalist agencies was to pretend that standard 30- and 60-second TV spots didn't exist nor did traditional magazine advertising.

DUFFY We've seen so many unique things that you've done with this campaign. It sounds like those might have been a result of the brief.

BOGUSKY It was.

MARTIN It really was part of the brief. I actually told the agencies that I did not want to see TV concepts. Don't present them. Then I said, "other than that, the net is wide open." The cool thing is that that's really how CP+B thinks. They don't think in terms of advertising. They think in terms of creative content. When we heard that, we said, "That's exactly what MINI needs." But it can't be creative content that only reaches small amounts of people. It's bigger than what many people might consider to be guerrilla marketing because we need creative content that's going to help us sell 25,000 cars.

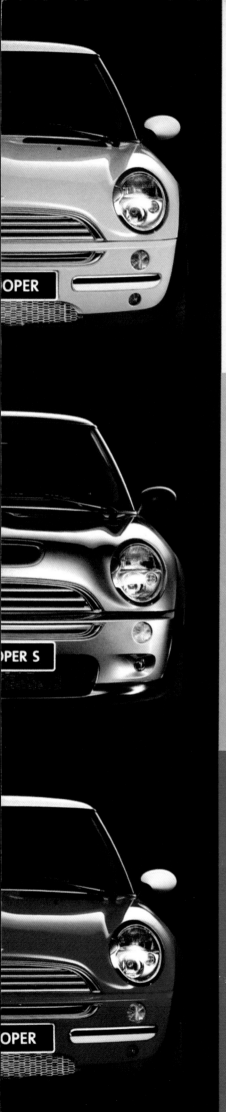

LET'S SIP, NOT GUZZLE.

Let's leave the off-road vehicles off road. Let's not use the size of our vehicle to make up for other shortcomings. Let's reclaim our garage space. Let's be nimble. Let's be quick. Let's be honest.

LET'S MOTOR.™

LET'S MASTER THE ASPHALT ARTS.

Let's hug the corner. Let's kiss the corner. Heck, let's marry the corner. Let's clip an apex. Let's make graceful lane changes. Let's create our own techniques. Let's teach them unto others. **LET'S MOTOR.™**

LET'S BURN THE MAPS.

Let's get lost. Let's turn right when we should turn left. Let's read fewer car ads and more travel ads. Let's eat when hungry. Let's drink when thirsty. Let's break routines, but not make a routine of it.

LET'S MOTOR.™

MINI COOPER S

in the front seat. Let's sit in
the driveway. Let's take the
keys out of the ignition.
Let's rest heads on headrests.
LET'S MOTOR.™

DUFFY Obviously, this required a different kind of team. Would you tell us a little bit about the team and how it came together?

MARTIN The first challenge was that MINI was a completely new brand within the BMW organization. Early on we had to set parameters and define what the brand was and how the brand was different. That was very important. One of the first things we did was to put together what we called an "inverting" campaign. We had a challenge to motivate a large part of the organization that we call "leveraged resources" people who work on MINI as well as other brands within the BMW Group. It was our responsibility to educate these people, to convince them that this brand was going to be a success, and to raise the enthusiasm level very early on so that we could garner the support of the entire organization.

We put together this invertising program. It was low cost but very high impact. Leading up to the launch, we gave everyone holiday gifts that we called magical motoring balls. These were "Eight Balls" customized with motoring sayings like: "Buy a hat at a truck stop," "Keep motoring," and "Order

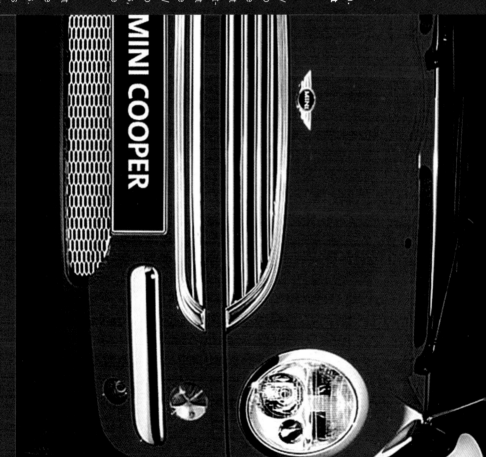

LET'S MOTOR.

We'd be remiss not to mention the long cut, or "scenic route," another well respected maxim of the motorer. Most long cuts include a series of twisties that will take you back to the glory days of rallying at Monte Carlo when MINI's classic predecessor took home the top honors in '64, '65 and '67.

GOLIATH LOST.

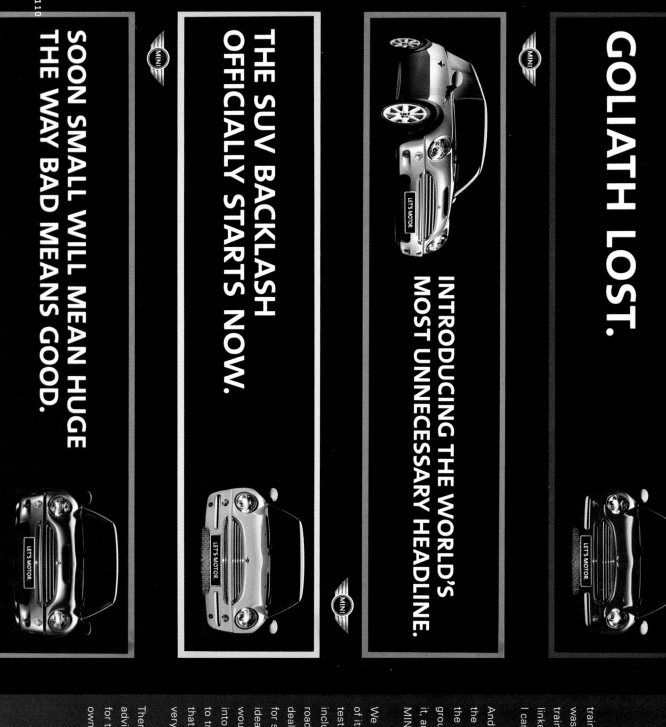

INTRODUCING THE WORLD'S MOST UNNECESSARY HEADLINE.

THE SUV BACKLASH OFFICIALLY STARTS NOW.

SOON SMALL WILL MEAN HUGE THE WAY BAD MEANS GOOD.

LET'S MOTOR

training materials by the branding group and vice versa. It was one of the biggest learning experiences for me — that training is just critical. Absolutely critical. And to have training linked to marketing and the brand team is the only way to go. I can't imagine it any other way.

And many of the ideas came from CP+B as well. Some of the generated ideas needed to find reasons for being, like the magical motoring ball, so I guess you could say it was a group effort. From there, we started to have some fun with it, and the whole idea of motoring ignited. This really became MINI's point of difference.

We did things like reduce a company newsletter to a quarter of its normal size to introduce the MINI. We did an employee test drive and a road tour to make sure the regions were included, because that's really where the rubber hits the road — their day-to-day contacts with the dealer. We took our dealers on an international dealer drive to Lisbon and London for some meetings where we introduced them to the whole idea of motoring and set the stage for what our expectations would be and how we were going to launch this new brand into the U.S. We treated them exactly how we wanted them to treat their customers. We introduced them to magazines that perhaps they wouldn't normally subscribe to but were very MINI-esque.

There was even more beyond that — sales ideas for motoring advisors; MotoringGear; CRM ideas, like how to make waiting for the delivery fun; new owner delivery packages; an on-line owners lounge; and more...

DUFFY I believe that often it's those nontraditional things that bring people closer to the brand. It shows how much the brand cares when every last detail is attended to. But it's not always easy to cover all those bases. Alex, what about your team? As we've discussed, so much of the work goes beyond traditional advertising. How are you set up in order to deliver?

BOGUSKY We're actually set up really traditionally. Our process with MINI is just something that organically happened. If you work in any agency, you know that the creative directors are usually beating on people for what they call "below the line" ideas. Everyone wants to do TV and print. We were thinking about things a little bit differently but still forcing it in many ways. I was asking people to give me more, to try something different. We started seeing success in campaigns where many of the things weren't TV or print. That's when we really felt a cultural shift in the agency. People began to see that their fame might be connected to something that's not so typical. And once that happened, it's been really organic.

DUFFY Do you attribute this kind of thinking to on-the-job training? Or, do you hire based on different criteria than a traditional advertising profile?

BOGUSKY It's a combination of both. Some of the schools are actually trying to teach kids to do this. In many ways it's made it more difficult for me to hire. Since now it's part of the curriculum, you don't know whether it's something that is natural to that person and something that they get turned on by, or whether it's "a part of the assignment."

There also seems to be some kind of trend in the industry — a counter-advertising trend, I guess. We seem to find that people are attracted to our shop because they're looking for even the smallest indication that somebody is doing something different. So we've found a fair number of people who've really just arrived at our door.

DUFFY   When you work on a project like the MINI campaign, do you put creative "specialists" on the job or do you ask everybody to come up with ideas?

BOGUSKY   We don't really have many "specialists." We have some teams that I would call vibe teams — where their ideas elicit as much of a feeling as specific communication does. But other than that, I wouldn't say we have specialists.

Over time I've found that the person you think will find the solution is the one who won't necessarily crack it. Instead, you'll find the answer from a surprising place. It happens over and over and over. I don't necessarily look at teams to be good at any particular thing. I find that we often crack the code in a counterintuitive way. I think to myself, "This team would be strange for that, let's give them a try…"

Interestingly, that kind of thinking is very different from the thinking that often happens on the client side. One of the first things many clients ask for is "somebody who has experience." I think in this business, there's incredible strength in ignorance. I always worry about losing the objectivity that comes with naiveté. Unfortunately, it's one of those things that many clients have completely backwards.

DUFFY I agree. Some of our best work has been in categories where we have done nothing in the category before nor known anything about the category. I find that it's in those instances that you think beyond the parameters of what's been done. And, that's when really great thinking happens.

BOGUSKY Right. It helps you to be able to see. One of the things that we talk about a lot is that it's almost impossible to see what's really going on. It's difficult to back out from a category far enough so that you can really see how that category plays within the culture. We're always doing things to try and trick ourselves into seeing something, like a visitor might see it.

DUFFY That's obviously one of the reasons why the campaign is so incredibly fresh. Was the client on board from the outset in terms of doing things that haven't been done before and creating a whole new position within the car culture?

BOGUSKY Yes. Kerri Martin was — in her own words — untraditional. It makes sense for MINI, especially because the car is untraditional. In general, you want not just your communications but everything you do, including the selection of media, to match the brand profile. So what we always talk about with the campaign is, "Don't say it; prove it." It's an innovative car, but we never want the copy to say, "This is an innovative car." You have to show it. The marketing has to have that same spirit that the vehicle has.

MANUAL OF MOTORING

MINIUSA.COM

ADDITIONAL READING:

On the Road, Jack Kerouac

Roadfood: 500 Diners, Farmland Buffets, Lobster Shacks, Pie Palaces and Other All-American Eateries, Jane & Michael Stern

There's No Toilet Paper on the Road Less Traveled: The Best of Travel Humor, Landy

Fodor's Flashmaps of NY, Washington D.C., Chicago & San Francisco

Fodor's How to Pack, Laurel Cardone

BOOKS ON TAPE

Road Rage Relaxation, Dean Montalbano

⚠ NOTE: MEDITATION TAPE ONLY. NOT FOR USE WHILE MOTORING.

WEBSITE

MINIUSA.COM For additional reading, building your own MINI or locating the dealer near you.

114

LET'S MOTOR

LET'S COMMUNICATE

Index Finger Salute
Subtle. Sublime. "Sup"

Peace Sign

Thumbs Up

Motorer's Oath of Honor

The Wave

Tap on the Roof

Winking the Lights

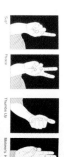

LET'S ATTRACT ATTENTION

Unconventional Use of Headlamps

LET'S STASH STUFF

2. Low Caddy

3. Door Caddy

4. Pizza Storage

5. Toll Ticket Caddy

How to Fit a Bike

LET'S PARK

The Phantom Spot

LET'S CUSTOMIZE

MINI Roof Graphics

Motoring Accessories

CUSTOMIZING YOUR MINI

Assembly:

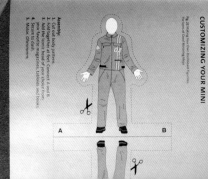

THE SHORTCUT IS THE SECRET PATH TO MOTORING.

Look for shortcuts. Always take a chance on finding a secret path. The best time to find a shortcut is on Sunday, when most people are still sleeping. There's less traffic, so you can take your time. A great shortcut can't be rushed. Warning: never look for new shortcuts on your way to work. This can be stressful and that's not what motoring is about.

THE BADGES OF THE MOTORER

When you motor properly, there'll be dirt around the tires, dust on the bonnet and bugs on the grille. Consider these signs of motoring. Wear them with pride. Of course, it's fun to wash your MINI, too. Just don't be in such a hurry to erase your experiences. Remember, a memento doesn't have to be a snow globe or a beer stein. It just has to remind you of a moment in time. And when birds happen to leave their mark on your MINI, try not to be too mad. It's inevitable. After all, the world is their in-flight lavatory.

MASTER THE ASPHALT ARTS.

Motorers strive to be accomplished commanders of their MINIs. Of course, they're not born with the gift. Moves have to be practiced. Skills must be honed. While average drivers shy away from parallel parking, motorers jump at the chance. It's an opportunity to shine – to be so dead-on accurate that people on the sidewalk toss them a compliment.

THE BOOK OF MOTORING

MINI

LET'S ENJOY
THE SMELL OF OUR CAR.

Unscented

Directions: Get some string or maybe dental floss. Slip it through the hole. Tie a loop. Hang from a rearview mirror. And there you have it.

MARTIN You know, it's not often that you get to start with a totally blank slate, but we did. The great thing is that the management of our company actually challenged us to think of different ways of doing things. They supported it. It wasn't just my team running off with the agency saying, "We're going to be renegades and do something different." The fact that the challenge came from the top of the organization was an opportunity for this company to do things differently and stretch the envelope. And it was a big responsibility at the same time.

We've seen the success as a result. As of September 2001 in the U.S., we had zero-percent unaided brand awareness and 12% aided, if you can believe it, vs. 85% in the U.K. and the rest of Europe, where the MINI was somewhat of an icon. In June 2003, we had 50% aided awareness. And, we're having fun as well.

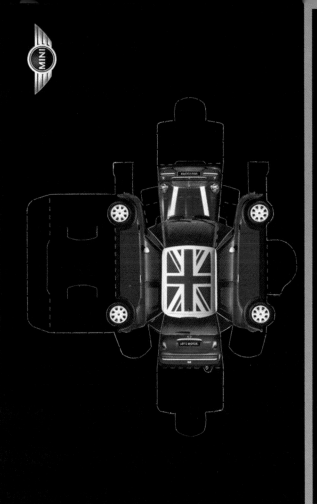

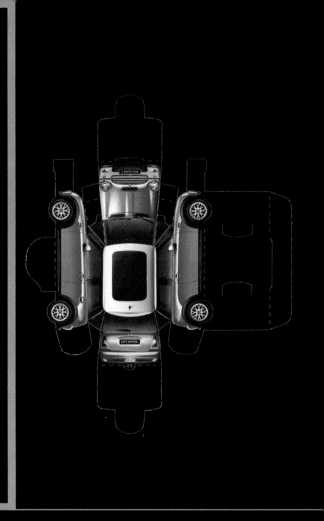

LET'S PARK IT ON OUR DESK. Let's drag race our favorite pen. Let's blow past the tape dispenser. Let's avoid coffee spills. Let's not get pulled over by our boss. Let's get lost in the office. On a 1/56th scale - **LET'S MOTOR.™**

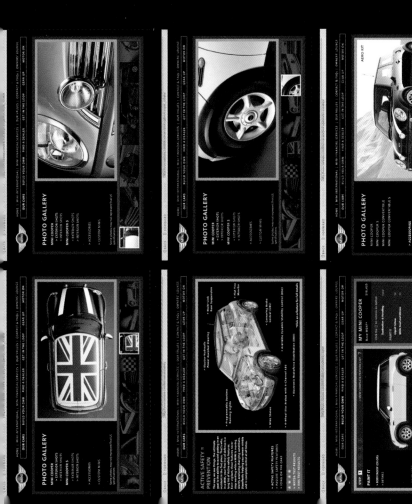

WHAT'S YOUR ANTI-DRUG?

CHALLENGE As a government-run public service effort, The Partnership For A Drug-Free America watched its message splinter in the hands of an increasing number of agency Good Samaritans.

SOLUTION Create a brand that serves as a delivery mechanism for a single voice that avoids preaching to kids by talking with them, engaging them, and inviting them to share their interests and passions online.

RESULT The phrase "What's Your Anti-drug?" diligently united multi-agency efforts and swiftly entered the American vernacular. Teens flooded the servers at whatsyourantidrug.com with personal essays and drawings that shared their everyday reasons for choosing not to use drugs.

BRIAN COLLINS senior partner, executive creative director [BRAND INTEGRATION GROUP]

VANESSA HARMATZ partner, management supervisor [OGILVY & MATHER]

DON MAPLE former senior policy analyst [THE WHITE HOUSE OFFICE OF NATIONAL DRUG CONTROL POLICY]

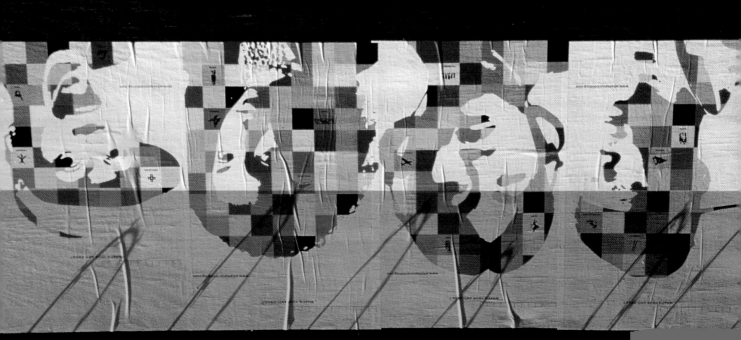

JOE DUFFY Historically, there are a number of public service campaigns that tried to convince kids to stay off drugs, but none of them were attached to a brand. How did the notion of creating a brand, as opposed to yet another stand-alone campaign, come to life?

BRIAN COLLINS We were asked to solve a larger strategic problem. The Office of National Drug Control Policy (ONDCP) and Partnership for a Drug-Free America speak to many different people, across many different platforms, and through work created by many different advertising agencies. We tried to find an idea that would build greater critical mass for all the varied work that the ONDCP funds. We had to find a solution that was specific enough to be identifiable and understood by kids. But the idea had to be open-ended enough so that each of the agencies that volunteered their

time, passion, and money could also have creative ownership of their own work. If we gave the agencies an idea that was too specific or narrow, they would not have been motivated to do their best work. It was a tough nut to crack at first.

COLLINS We have a terrific planning and ethnography group, and they really inspired us. So at the start, I put all of our strategic and creative thinkers in a room together. Then we shared stories about what it was like when we were all teens. We quickly found powerful common themes to play with.

VANESSA HARMATZ We also did a lot of research with kids. We learned that they were really tired of being preached at and being told what to do. But each kid in every focus group said they had something they felt really passionate about. It's not just a word or thing; it's something that was a huge piece of their life—something that drove them forward. So our solution needed to have a lot of flexibility to accommodate each kid, but also be specific enough so that it could unify everything that ONDCP was doing. These are characteristics of a great brand.

DUFFY How is a team put together on a mega-campaign like this? Does someone decide you need an ad team, a design team and a planner?

COLLINS It changes. In this case, the agency co-presidents Bill Gray and Rick Boyko came to me after a big meeting with General Barry McCaffrey (at the time the head of the ONDCP). They told me we needed to come up with a unifying brand idea that could hold together all the ONDCP's efforts aimed at youth. As we normally do here, we saw it as a

freedom

dating

KAPOW!

comic books

larger opportunity and started asking bigger questions. At the beginning of a project, my team helps craft the big brand idea—and then we develop analogous visual metaphors, design and creative languages. And that's what we did here. And we started pulling all the visual language stuff together very quickly.

DUFFY Was McCaffrey the ultimate decision maker on the client side?

COLLINS Yes. General McCaffrey was the catalyst for the project and the key person we presented to in Washington, D.C. He is the general. He looks and sounds like a general. People practically stand and salute. He is quite articulate about what he wants to make happen.

band

math

life

baseball

knowledge

hip-hop

DUFFY Did the phrase, "Anti-Drug," come from the kids in the focus groups, or was it inspired by what the kids had to say?

COLLINS The expression "anti-drug campaign" was already out there. So we leveraged part of that. We did a lot of talking internally about the things that kept us off drugs when we were kids, too. What inspired us and kept us out of trouble? We quickly discovered that everyone who stayed out of real trouble had a big passion. Whether it was comic books, track, singing, football, or French Club, it fueled their soul in some meaningful way. Not only did it make them feel more alive, it helped them build character and become more disciplined. My creative partner Charles Hall came in one morning after one of our long conversations and taped a sheet of paper on my office door. It said, "My anti-drug is fashion. My anti-drug is music. My anti-drug is football. What's your anti-drug?" I thought we found our answer.

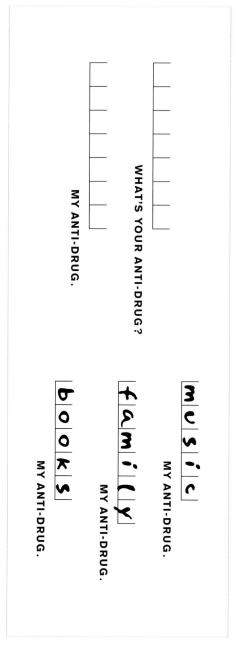

WHAT'S YOUR ANTI-DRUG?

music MY ANTI-DRUG.

family MY ANTI-DRUG.

books MY ANTI-DRUG.

HARMATZ Three years later, the phrase has become a part of the American vernacular. It's in *The New York Times*. We hear kids saying it. The phrase started as a brand idea, and now it's part of kids' everyday language.

DUFFY Because it's so focused and yet open-ended enough to continue in many different ways across all forms of communication.

COLLINS I thought that was a perfect idea. So we worked to come up with a visual program to bring it all together. Designer Baruch Gorkin had just returned from a trip overseas, and he had to fill out a long customs form. Knowing that we were working on this puzzle, he showed us how we might use something similar to the empty little blocks on those forms as a fill-in-the-blank solution for "What's Your Anti-Drug?" It created an open-ended system for kids to fill in themselves.

DUFFY Tell me about the work you say you quickly pulled together. Did "What's Your Anti-Drug?" become the glue for all the campaigns?

COLLINS Absolutely. Once we rephrased "Anti-Drug" into a provocative question, soon after we believed it could be the conceptual platform for all communications. Our idea was not to tell kids what to do. No more "Just Say No." Instead, our idea was to pose a question that could open up a bigger, more inspiring dialogue. We presumed that kids were already intelligent enough to know they had the answers to combat drugs. So rather than tell them what to do in a pedantic way, we invited the kids themselves into the question. Once the campaign began, they sent their poetry, their drawings, their films, and their music to the Web site—anything that they could show to demonstrate their anti-drug. And the partner agencies turned many of their suggestions into commercials.

DUFFY Did you present your work in type comp so it looked finished, or did you show rough sketches?

COLLINS My team and I (Charles Hall, Baruch Gorkin and Patrik Bolecek) took the work as far as we could. It was nearly finished. We needed to show the ONDCP how the work would really look in *Teen People*, on a billboard in Chicago, at a high school in Massachusetts, or wild postings in New York City. We were quite thorough, so Don Maple or General McCaffery wouldn't be forced to take any unnecessary leaps of faith about how it would work.

DUFFY Don, tell me how you collaborated with the Ogilvy team. How did you come to agreement on the best way to visualize this idea?

DON MAPLE The short answer is, we listened to our agency. Ogilvy not only brought us a concept, they brought us a

plan to determine the best media for the idea. This even included the promotion plans to launch the whole project. I have to tell you, we loved it from the very beginning and went along with pretty much everything they proposed.

In working with Partnership for a Drug-Free America, we have had advertising in one form or another done by more than 60 agencies. Ogilvy's idea to create a brand that works as a unifying factor, a common denominator for all of our work, has been a crucial feature to the whole campaign.

HARMATZ It was a very complex 360-degree campaign. We needed to explain how this idea would be executed across each and every medium. We needed to create a Web site, a postcard, 1-800 numbers to capture call-ins, even a clearinghouse to receive the postcards from kids who sent their artwork and submissions. We expressed that our plan would require an incredible amount of collaboration.

COLLINS We also explained how we could do outreach programs at junior high and high school tennis courts, basketball courts, and football fields. We wanted to show how we could make this thing seep into culture without appearing pedantic. And how to make it feel cool and motivating so kids would want to participate in it.

DUFFY What made you decide on one medium over another?

HARMATZ We thought about an average kid's day. He goes to school, he gets the message from an in-school medium, but then goes to a movie and he sees a lobby poster. He goes to his favorite skate shop and picks up a postcard. He goes outside and sees an outdoor board, and at the YMCA he sees it again. It reaches him every step of the way. Where he works, lives, plays.

COLLINS One of the first things we did was negotiate with

WHAT'S YOUR ANTI-DRUG?

hip-hop
knowledge
breakin'
baseball
life
self-respect
community
film
karate
yo-yos
family
leadership
art
pride
role models
bowling
nature
tv
running
ping-pong
yoga
fitness
hangin'
www.
dogs
shoes
records
pets
loungin'
piano
confidence
sci-fi
surfing
mountain biking
cheerleading
house
drama

cycling

rock

sci-fi

brotherhood

peace

faith

biology

friendship

shopping

reading

debate team

groovin'

writing

dj

family

kissing

games

gardening

computers

role models

motorcycles

basketball

dreams

freedom

snowboarding

rap

model cars

sports

cars

sewing

soccer

neighborhood

gymnastics

strength

tribe

thinking

got bello... than...

877.958.3900 or go to

atsyourantidrug.com

he details and

ructions.

much respect.

stay strong.

cinemas around the country to put some of these posters in the place of, say, a Harry Potter poster. So, the posters actually ran in "coming attraction" kiosks. I remember being at a small movie theater in Minneapolis. A mom was talking to her son. He might have been 12 or so. The poster apparently initiated a conversation and the mother asked her son, "What is your anti-drug?" and the kid started to talk about how much he loved to draw. The conversation happened right there in front of me. It was exactly what we wanted to inspire. We wanted to find a way to validate those things that truly move kids. Healthy, personal activities and passions that engage their hearts.

DUFFY With your audience, the online component is a critical vehicle, not only for collecting information, but also for staying in tune with the kids. Who was responsible for that part of the equation, and how did they

collaborate with the rest of the teams and clients?

HARMATZ Ogilvy Interactive. They worked very closely with the big group and with the ONDCP to create a fully interactive Web site where kids could actually see the other kids' work and submit their own work to the site. Or they could simply submit a word or phrase. We had an ongoing tally of how many kids had submitted work to the site. So it was very interactive; it was very real-time. Kids could see the results of their own collective efforts.

DUFFY Don, what do you do to maintain consistency between different agencies and new campaigns? Do you have a set of guidelines?

MAPLE Yes, we have a specifications manual that lays down specific graphic requirements. Everybody has to follow it.

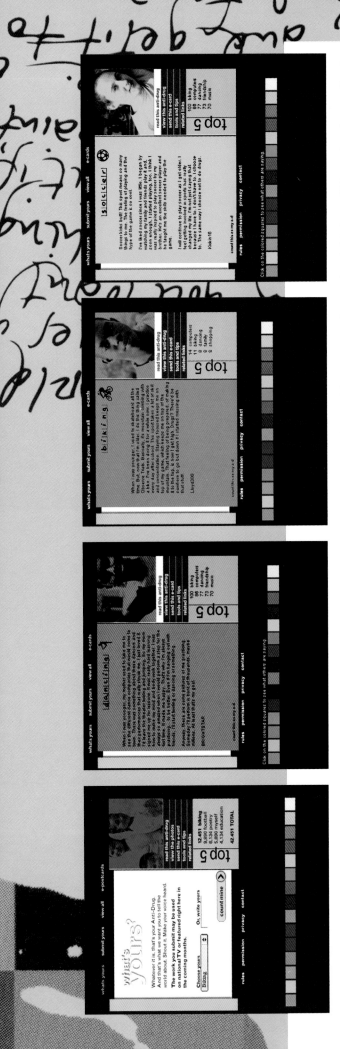

But it's a very flexible brand. There is a good deal of room for the creative team to build the brand identity into their work. In fact, I think the flexibility of the brand and its ability to evolve with the campaign is remarkable.

Initially, the campaign focused on a target we call tweens—the 11- to 13-year-old group. As the campaign evolved, we refocused it on an older group, 14- to 16-year-olds, who we found to be a little bit deeper in terms of their experimentation with drugs. The differences between the two groups meant a difference in everything about the creative. We found it was not difficult to transform the brand right along with the change in age focus. So the brand lives on, evolving very nicely with each campaign.

DUFFY There's a wide range of iconography and visual components to the campaign. Did you test them with your audience and then compile the most powerful elements in order to create this brand iconography?

COLLINS The first thing we do on any kind of integrated assignment is to look at the context in which our communication is going to appear. We looked at every kind of visual expression in the culture: magazines, television, newspapers, advertising, Web sites, posters. We literally covered walls in our office trying to understand common conceptual themes. We found that most of it, particularly stuff done by advertising agencies, was really dumbed down. It was as if they believed the only stuff kids looked at was either really ugly or distressed grunge. We believed there could be a different language—a smarter way to talk to kids. A language that was clean, optimistic, and bright. Beautiful, even.

DUFFY On one hand, it's incredibly cool and appealing to this very young audience. But at the same time, it's optimistic and bright. And sophisticated.

COLLINS We wanted to create a visual language that the ONDCP could call its own, and at the same time, would speak to kids in a sincere way. So it wouldn't look like ONDCP was trying to repurpose youth culture and just slap their logo on it.

HARMATZ When you look at the work, you see icons that are a real representation of what kids said in groups. Plus, you see real kids, not dressed-up Hollywood kids.

COLLINS I think that was important. We wanted to create a visual solution that we could deploy across other expressions. My interactive partner Mach Arom and I believed the

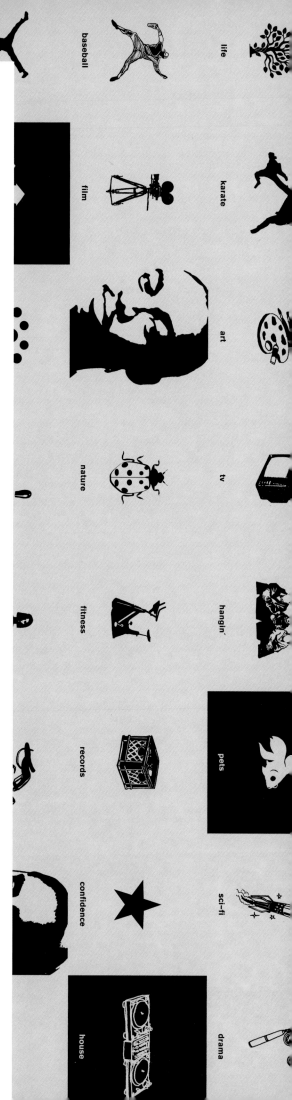

life

karate

art

tv

hangin´

pets

sci-fi

drama

baseball

film

nature

fitness

records

confidence

house

DUFFY Has the brand spread its tentacles throughout the country? Or are there saturation markets and markets where you've hardly scratched the surface?

COLLINS Within the first year, 67% of the school kids we targeted could recognize the "What's Your Anti-Drug?" visual tag, appreciate it, and understand the proposition. I think the test of a branding idea is how deeply it seeps into popular culture. And this shows up in everyday dialogue with kids. And that seemed to happen within less than a year after the launch of the campaign. I think that's a good proof point.

DUFFY Don, where do you expand the brand from here to get more kids involved, get more hits on the site, and get more content developed?

MAPLE I believe this brand's equity and its ubiquity in everyday language is so valuable that we would be crazy to abandon it. And there's no plan to do that whatsoever. The nature of its evolution is something that we would put as a

squares we used in the posters, for example, might become interactive and animated. So now you can click on them and you find out about skateboarding, ballet, comic books, whatever. The interactive team got all excited about this and built on it. We made a solution together that worked in print, tv, outdoor and online.

HARMATZ Kids could also go to a mall and literally write on a 10-foot by 40-foot grid. They could sign it and write their Anti-Drug on the wall right next to some other kid's.

COLLINS They could also do that on the Web site, freevibe. com. Launching a brand idea like this and using a Web site as the primary fulfillment mechanism was a difficult challenge. After all, you can't expect millions of kids across this country to flock to an anti-drug Web site. It's just not what kids do. Yet, they did. And they came to it in droves, evidently. Despite this sort of unnatural act, freevibe.com still gets about a half-million visits a month.

challenge to Brian, Vanessa, and all the agencies that give their time and talent. Most brands require growth, and we know that ours will as well. I'm very confident in the flexibility of the brand. And I think it will be able to sustain all sorts of evolutionary changes.

DUFFY A great idea is one that can constantly evolve. It has to grow and expand to reflect culture as it changes. Any subsequent work can follow the lead of that great idea. That said, I find it disheartening that in our business, many great ideas that serve to establish one voice for a brand are nibbled at until they become something unrecognizable.

COLLINS It is. What I've learned in my time here is the amount of evangelizing you have to do to convince people to protect an idea. You have to persuade and constantly remind people that there is room in your idea for them to do something extraordinary.

breaki

knowled

hip-ho

128

WHAT'S YOUR ANTI-DRUG?

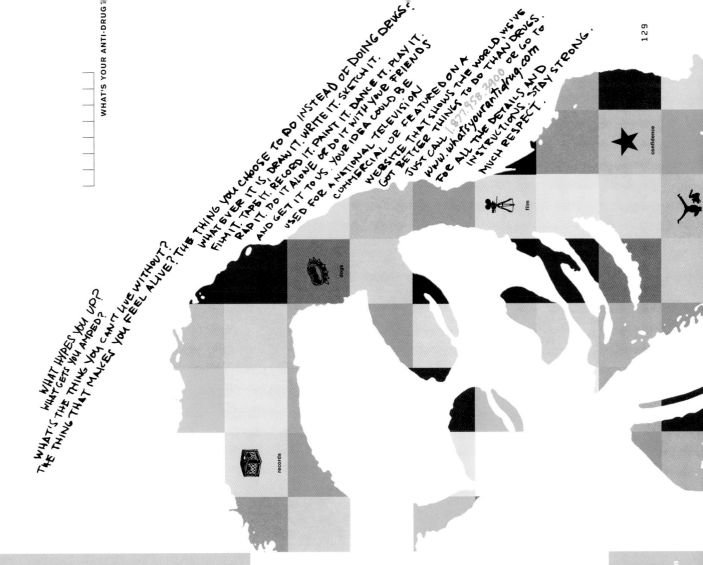

WHAT HYPES YOU UP?
WHAT GETS YOU AMPED?
WHAT'S THE THING YOU CAN'T LIVE WITHOUT?
THE THING THAT MAKES YOU FEEL ALIVE? THE THING YOU CHOOSE TO DO INSTEAD OF DOING DRUGS?
WHATEVER IT IS, DRAW IT. WRITE IT. SKETCH IT.
FILM IT. TAPE IT. RECORD IT. PAINT IT. DANCE IT. PLAY IT.
RAP IT. DO IT ALONE OR DO IT WITH YOUR FRIENDS.
AND GET IT TO US. YOUR IDEA COULD BE
USED FOR A NATIONAL TELEVISION
COMMERCIAL OR FEATURED ON A
WEBSITE THAT SHOWS THE WORLD WE'VE
GOT BETTER THINGS TO DO THAN DRUGS.
JUST CALL 1.877.958.3400 OR GO TO
www.whatsyourantidrug.com
FOR ALL THE DETAILS AND
INSTRUCTIONS. STAY STRONG.
MUCH RESPECT.

records

dogs

film

confidence

129

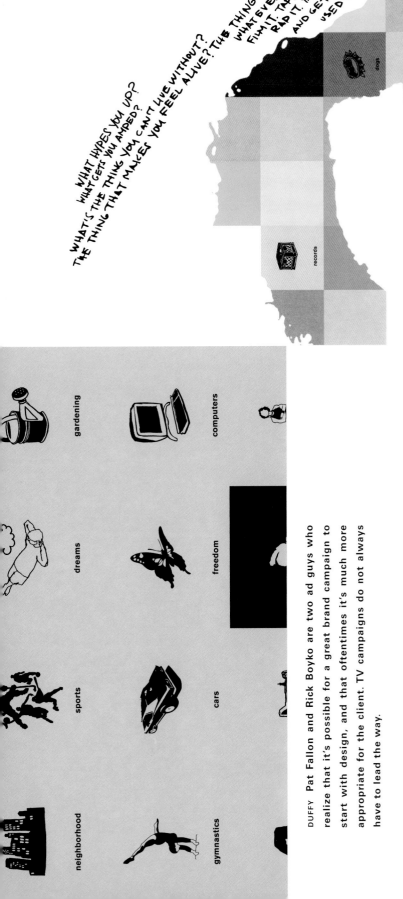

gardening

computers

dreams

freedom

sports

cars

neighborhood

gymnastics

DUFFY Pat Fallon and Rick Boyko are two ad guys who realize that it's possible for a great brand campaign to start with design, and that oftentimes it's much more appropriate for the client. TV campaigns do not always have to lead the way.

COLLINS I agree. I love the next big hit :30 spot, but I think creating a big branding idea requires a different skill set beyond commercial making. Sometimes a big idea comes from people whose passion is creating great TV, but it just as easily comes from people whose passion is design first. From people who like to create visual solutions to address a business problem. And the best brand solutions are, in the end, often design-driven solutions.

www.whatsyourantidrug.com

STARBUCKS

CHALLENGE How do you define success with new audiences? Through new distribution channels; with a package form with the disadvantage of being half the size of its many competitors; and "coffee in a can" sending unbranded poor-taste cues to consumers?

SOLUTION Find a connection point with consumers that is true to the product, speaks with quality and allows the brand to stretch to new markets and new customers.

RESULT Sell-in goals exceeded. Positioning accomplished with rifle-shot accuracy, allowing the Starbucks brand to increase sales and solidify share leadership in a fragmenting category.

AMY WIRTANEN director of bakery and food strategy [NORTH AMERICAN COFFEE PARTNERSHIP]

KEVIN RODDY former creative director [FALLON WORLDWIDE]

DAVID MASHBURN designer [DUFFY NEW YORK]

JOE DUFFY Can you tell us about how you approached the brief so that it was conducive to collaboration between the advertising guys and the design guys?

AMY WIRTANEN That was really a very simple problem for me to solve on this project. The agencies were in the same family and that made it easy to make the briefing process a collaborative one. The brief considered everything we were going to have to do from the outset and integrated everyone into the entire process. Ultimately, the involvement of both advertising and design drove all the communications behind this product. Whether it was packaging or advertising, it didn't matter because there was one brief and one team.

DUFFY Did you use a different approach on this project versus others you've worked on?

WIRTANEN The biggest difference on this project was in the way we were able to reach consensus without the normal hurdles. When you think about the team that had to come to consensus, it's really quite extraordinary. The Starbucks DoubleShot effort was a joint venture with two different parent companies involved in all direction and decisions. Then, there were consultants from Starbucks' design group. And, we had the regular structure within the joint venture of the North American Coffee Partnership itself — a general

manager, myself, the director of marketing, so on and so forth. It was a huge team that had to come together and decide on a singular direction. Just the mere fact that we were able to accomplish that is extraordinary to me.

I think the reason we were able to reach consensus was that we kept it really simple. We made sure from the very beginning we had a clear direction for this project. There wasn't a lot of confusion about what this product would be and how it would live within the brand portfolio. We knew it had to be different from anything out there. We also understood exactly whom this product was going to be for and why they were going to be interested in it. It was really tight from the very beginning and again, that goes back to getting all the right people involved early on.

DUFFY Was there a proven process you followed to integrate the players and develop the work?

KEVIN RODDY It was an interesting process from the beginning. We presented at least two rounds of advertising development before we decided to take a different approach. In those first couple of rounds, we just couldn't hit it. In hindsight, I think it's really because the epicenter of this whole thing is Starbucks and Starbucks isn't a brand that is about advertising in any traditional sense of the word. We really

couldn't approach it like traditional advertising, but much of the work we had on the table in the early rounds did just that. They looked like ads. It just wasn't right. It wasn't right for the brand. And frankly, it wasn't taking full advantage of the great branding that had been done in the development of the Starbucks DoubleShot identity.

So when we went into another round, I decided to try something different and put together a team of designers and a writer and ask them to think about how they might solve the ad challenge. They came back with an idea that I felt was very much in the bull's eye of where the Starbucks brand ought to be.

DAVID MASHBURN We approached it like a design problem and just looked at it in the same way we would look at any other project. First, we understood that Starbucks is a brand with a very specific look and feel. It has a specific palette of colors and textures that are inherently "Starbuckian." It has its own unique language. In itself, it is its own little world.

We decided to capitalize on that idea — literally. So we created a unique world that would allow Starbucks Double-Shot and Frappuccino to live their own way. This idea gave us an incredible amount of flexibility in terms of what this stuff would look like and how we could even make it feel less like

advertising and a lot more like Starbucks.

DUFFY And what about the process for direction and approvals?

WIRTANEN This was completely new and different. It was the first new product since the introduction of Frappuccino in 1996. We were really breaking new ground. In a lot of ways I broke the rules in order to get this done. A lot of what we did was done under the radar of the typical structured approval process. Ultimately, we were able to get it done because the people on the team passionately believed in this project. That passion helped us open doors and make things happen.

DUFFY The look of the campaign is very compatible with the Starbucks brand feeling, yet it was a departure from much of the advertising that had been done in the past.

WIRTANEN Yes, you're right, especially the idea of animation and the general look and feel. They were so distinctive that this effort could be seen as a bit of a departure. But the reason we ultimately went with animation is because it felt more Starbuckian.

DUFFY What do you mean by more Starbuckian?

STARBU
double
– Espresso &

PREMIUM COFF

6.5 FL OZ (1

137

COFFE

STARBU

WIRTANEN More Starbuckian. You know, right for our brand. It felt true to the brand. It was a nod to all of our audiences. I think it was a nod to what was happening in the marketplace at that time.

MASHBURN What we loved about this look was that it was very unique and simple and still felt right for the Starbucks brand. Much of the inspiration for the style, as well as the final production, was the result of inspiration from and collaboration with Psyop, a New York production house. We wanted a different look. We wanted it to make people take notice and pause; yet at the same time, we wanted them to feel comfortable that it was coming from Starbucks. It is common for companies to randomly attach style to their brand and to miss the mark. I feel that this work did a great job in capturing a feeling that was right on for the Starbucks brand.

DUFFY It's interesting to see how the rest of the campaign evolved beyond television. How did that all come about?

RODDY I had this thought when I saw the initial television idea. It reminded me of old spirits posters. I thought, couldn't we make ads that aren't really ads but more like posters? Something so beautiful that people would want to put them

up. Something that doesn't feel like an ad so much but maybe more like a beautiful piece of art. The designers really latched on to this idea and started doing a lot of research and investigation. They asked Psyop to get involved, which brought another perspective into the mix — a whole different kind of brain.

I have to give all the players a lot of credit because in the end this didn't feel like advertising. It didn't look like advertising. It was very Starbuckian, and it really hit the bull's eye of who they are as a brand.

DUFFY Did they take to this approach as being Starbuckian right off the bat, or did it require some convincing or revisions on your team's part?

RODDY No. I remember presenting it to Howard Schultz at Starbucks in Seattle. There wasn't a lot of set up. We had some great boards that were beautifully designed. He immediately latched on to the idea of creating this little world with this little man that lives on this planetary thing. He loved it. And if I recall correctly, he said, "I think that's great. Go make them."

We thought, great, this is very Starbuckian and Starbucks is on board, but will Pepsi like it? And they did. They really

did. They pushed us hard in the execution of it. And that was good. It made the end product even better than it might have been.

DUFFY **So if Starbucks thought it was right, what do you think the draw was for Pepsi?**

RODDY I don't know. I think they saw the Starbuckiness of it all. And I think they liked the non-traditional quality of it as well.

DUFFY **Did the trucks and the sampling ideas come after the fact or were those deliverables in the initial brief?**

RODDY All that came more after the fact. They really began to love the color palette and the animation style and this character. They began to see the opportunities and the value of it as a bigger branding idea. We pushed pretty hard, too. And we all agreed: "Let's make this more than just some ads."

MASHBURN As designers we are always trying to get people to think of how their brand might come to life in unexpected ways. Starbucks was willing and ready to put their brand in a non-traditional light.

DUFFY **Do you think the Yin/Yang approach to the adver-** tising campaign made this more complicated?

MASHBURN From a problem-solving perspective, yes, it did. But that was the brief. I find that the best work often comes from difficult challenges.

WIRTANEN The Yin/Yang was actually meant to solve a difficult communication challenge. We found that it actually served as a clarifying factor for consumers. We found that when you put DoubleShot next to Frappuccino, not only did people understand what DoubleShot was and how it was different from bottled Frappuccino, but they also got what bottled Frappuccino was and how it was different from DoubleShot.

DUFFY **Looking back, what was the best part of this project for you?**

WIRTANEN The best part was that it was like it was under a blessed moon or a blessed star. It all came together so seamlessly. I think it gets back to the team on this project. They knew what we had to communicate. And most important, they all loved what they were doing. If you ask them to this day, I bet everyone would say this project was one of their favorites. We had a lot of passionate people behind this project. It helped to make for a seamless process. Importantly, we had advocates all the way to the top.

All of that combined is what really made it such a successful introduction.

RODDY For me, one of the most interesting things was to see so clearly how differently advertising and design people think. They just come at problems in very different ways. As a creative director, I wish I could bottle the whole process, study it, and figure out how to do it myself because the result was very different. And that's just what we really needed at that point. Something not like a traditional advertising solution.

MASHBURN There were many firsts in this process — a new product, a different way of working (for everyone involved), a first in developing animated advertising for Fallon and Duffy. In the end, it really opened my mind to new ways to solve difficult challenges. It was a learning experience for the whole team. And we were so very fortunate to work with such passionate and talented people. The whole team deserves an enormous amount of credit. To date, this project ranks as one of my favorites.

WINTER X GAMES

CHALLENGE Small budgets. Limited media exposure. A marketing savvy and cynical target. An idea that many would consider risky and that had to make its way through corporate approvals.

SOLUTION Speak the language of the people you're talking to. Offer them something interesting. In general, remember that marketing doesn't qualify as "interesting" to them.

RESULT Communications that is more like art or entertainment than traditional marketing. The campaign found its way into the cultural buzz and lives of the audience.

KIM SCHOEN former associate creative director/art director [WIEDEN+KENNEDY NEW YORK]
LEE ANN DALY senior vice president marketing [ESPN]

145

Never Ski With Scissors

WINTER X GAMES ✚ Safety First

February 2 - 6 Mount Snow, Vermont ESPN ESPN2

PLAY THE WINTER X GAME ON EXPN.COM

February 2–6 Mount Snow, Vermont ESPN ESPN2 ABC

SUNDAY 02.04
ABC 1:00 – 2:30 PM ET
Snowmobiling SnoCross
Big Moto X
Men's Skier X

SUNDAY 02.04
ESPN 9:00 – 11:00 PM ET
Big Air Moto X

TUESDAY 02.06
ESPN 9:30 – 11:00 PM ET
Snowmobiling SnoCross
Men's Slopestyle Snowboarding
Men's Skier X
Big Air Moto X

ESPN 6:00 – 7:00 PM ET
Women's Slopestyle Snowboarding
Snowmobiling SnoCross

SATURDAY 02.03
ABC 5:00 – 6:00 PM ET
Men's Snowboarder X
Big Air Skiing
Snowmobiling SnoCross

FRIDAY 02.02
ESPN 9:00 – 11:00 PM ET
Women's Snowboarder X
Men's Snowboarder X
Big Air Skiing

SUNDAY 02.04
ESPN 9:00 – 11:00 PM ET
Big Air Moto X
Men's Super Pipe Snowboarding
Ultra Cross Skiing/Snowboarding
Snowmobiling HillCross

MONDAY 02.05
ESPN2 8:00 – 11:00 PM ET
Women's Big Air Snowboarding
Women's Skier X
Women's Super Pipe Snowboarding

TUESDAY 02.06
ESPN 9:00 – 11:00 PM ET
Men's Big Air Snowboarding
Snowmobiling HillCross
Big Air Moto X

JOE DUFFY Can you tell us about the brief for this project?

LEE ANN DALY It was, and it always is, to do something that represents what the Games are about. But to do it in such a way that people will talk about it, because the budget is quite small, particularly for Winter X.

KIM SCHOEN It was a very open brief. We really tried to reflect the target's take on the games and their countercultural nature. What we hoped to do was to help create culture rather than reflect the existing culture. We tried to add things visually and conceptually to give people something that could become part of their world — not only as advertising, but also as imagery. Like the stickers we produced. They found their way onto snowboards; and from there, the imagery all gets woven into the culture.

DALY Basically, we tried to do what was right for our audience. You have to push to make sure that you do something breakthrough and have people talk about it. It's particularly important because we don't have a lot of resources, especially off-channel resources, to support Winter X. We are always striving to create something that gets talk value. I think about it like this: Talk value is an exponent of creative—whatever the creative is and wherever it appears. If 20 people see it and talk about it, it keeps growing. And it continues to cascade until you find that there are 200,000 people talking about it. That's value. Talk value. Word of mouth.

It's about being pervasive, which is important when you have a tiny budget. You need to find ways to extend the message and do so creatively, across many different media.

February 2 – 6 Mount Snow, Vermont ESPN ESPN2

WINTER X GAMES ✚ Safety First

Do Not Stare Directly at the Sun

February 2 - 6 Mount Snow, Vermont ESPN ESPN2

✚ Safety First ✚ WINTER X GAMES

Keep Clear of Power Lines

February 2 - 6 Mount Snow, Vermont ESPN ESPN2

Safety First ✚ WINTER X GAMES

Do Not Drink Gasoline

DUFFY How about your thoughts on wanting to become a part of culture. Those are the types of things that don't come effortlessly, but they do deliver an integrated product. When people go in saying, "Our brief is to do something integrated," a lot of times it seems to be more difficult.

SCHOEN It's funny for me to think about it that way. We just wanted to reach the people who are involved in the X Games in all the ways that would be relevant to them.

DUFFY Which is perfect. These consumers are far from traditional in their media consumption.

DALY That's why I think the team decided to try to find something inside the "bros and pros" culture of action sports, as

we call them. The idea of "safety" and doing somewhat perverse things to gentle creatures all came together in a kind of dirty animation. When we saw it, we said, "Oh, that's really cool." It has its tongue planted firmly in cheek, because we really do worry about safety. The key is that the athletes embraced it and thought it was hilarious.

SCHOEN We knew we didn't want to do anything too realistic. We wanted to go over the top with silliness and even a gruesome quality. And the idea of safety was the interesting counterpoint. We had a concept. Then I saw some of Geoff McFetridge's artwork, and it just seemed like the perfect iteration because it rendered the concept harmless. It balanced the gore in a funny way. His style was a perfect embodiment of the concept. He's also done some great design in a number of areas, including Burton snowboards.

NEVER

SKI WITH SCISSORS

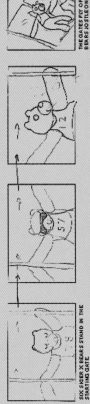

SIX SKIER X BEARS STAND IN THE STARTING GATE

THE GATES FLY OPEN AND THE BEARS JOSTLE ONE ANOTHER AS THEY PICK UP SPEED.

WE MOVE IN ON THE LEADER – HE IS HURLING DOWN THE MOUNTAIN HOLDING A PAIR OF SCISSORS.

HE'S SKIING LIKE A CHAMPION

HE'S CORNERING – HE'S JUMPING

THEN HE CATCHES AN EDGE

CUT TO THE BEARS POV – WE SEE THE SCISSORS COMING TOWARD HIM

Never Ski With Scissors

Safety First   Winter X Games

THE HEAD LANDS IN THE SNOW

IN THE BACKGROUND HIS BODY

CUT BACK TO A WIDE SHOT – WE

DUFFY So how did the campaign come together?

SCHOEN We worked collaboratively with Geoff. He has a very distinct style, and he created certain characters. For the ad concept, my partner Kevin Proudfoot and I came up with the ideas and some new characters. We went out to L.A. to work with Geoff and the characters came to life.

DUFFY Was it a conscious decision to develop a look that could live in a lot of different ways, or did it just start with the germ of an idea and then spread to all these different things?

SCHOEN I think that's what we liked about Geoff's artwork. It's sort of coveted. It seems everyone who sees something

of his wants it. Just to have it. And so that implies that it will work in any medium because it's very iconographic.

DALY You're right. It's almost like Marimekko sheets. I want to decorate my son's room with it. I really love it. We try to think that way now about everything we do. I love thinking about how we can take this and bring it to life in different ways. It's not so much about all the different ways that we would want to sell it as it is about all the different ways that a consumer would want it.

DUFFY It's simple. The work is beautifully designed. It's not your typical traditional advertising.

SCHOEN Geoff has a very wry sense of humor. I think it's the

combination of simplicity and a great graphic sensibility, with a strong sense of humor, that makes everybody want it.

DUFFY Was this project, and the way you approached it, significantly different from other campaigns you've developed?

SCHOEN Every time I work on the X Games, it's a relief because the brief is so open. It demands that you up the vanguard of visual thinking and everything you do because the audience is so sophisticated. It becomes a real challenge, and one that's always opening and freeing for me.

DUFFY One of the things we're focusing on is brands that speak through many different media, using many different

ty First

Winter X Games

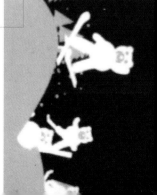

elements to create a singular voice. Is there anything about your approach that enabled you to achieve this focused perspective?

SCHOEN I think that when you have a good concept it has legs, and you know it because things come effortlessly. I didn't consciously decide that this was going to be an integrated campaign. In everything we do, we just assume people are going to want to see it in different forms, if it's a strong concept with strong design. But I do feel that things should be integrated and that the same message should be heard from every front. There's absolutely no other way to do it because otherwise it's confusing. There are too many messages out there. Simple and integrated is the only way I like to do things.

KIM SCHOEN At Wieden we don't like to do things that look like advertising, so our advertisements hopefully don't look like most ads. They have more in common with posters or things that you want to tack up and see all the time. I think because we're not designing or art directing in traditional advertising boxes to begin with, it's a natural outcropping that everything works in all mediums.

Winter X Games
February 2–6 Mount Snow, VT
ESPN ESPN2 ABC

Safety First

DUFFY **Lee Ann, are you involved in helping choose the teams at Wieden who work on your business? Do you ask for particular people based on their ability to cross the boundaries of media and applications?**

DALY No, but I can tell you that the most important qualification is that they are sports fans. Ideally they are fans of the particular sport they are creating work for. Then I know they are already part of the way there. They already understand the culture. I trust them to pick the right people, and they're masterful at it. This team in particular knew how to bravely find something that has absolutely nothing to do with sports, or even male-oriented design, and make it work.

DUFFY **I think that may be the recipe for success. Do something totally unexpected, and then it breaks through** — but it breaks through because it's totally unexpected as well as totally appropriate.

DALY That's it. In some cases you sit there and you smack your head and you think, "Oh, it's so obvious." And in some cases you smack your head and ask, "How did she do that?"

DUFFY **Can you tell us a little bit about how you measured the success of this campaign?**

DALY Talk value, I think, more than anything. I mean, we got a lot of people talking about it. A lot of people. We also did grassroots marketing and handed out stickers. You still see those in Manhattan all over the place. So I think that's probably a fairly decent measure of its impact. People interacted with it, adopted it, and had fun with it. We also had very very good ratings for those X Games. And people still talk about it.

SCHOEN One success story was when I was at the X Games. They were giving away prizes and one of them was a signed poster. The audience went crazy for it. It was in the snow, on a stage. To see how they all cheered when someone won the poster was a very thrilling moment for me.

DALY You get good work by letting it happen. You can quote me on that one.

Winter X Games

Safety First

Safety First

PAUL SMITH

CHALLENGE   After opening a small shop to sell collections of what he liked, ironically, Paul Smith's success threatened to restrict the individuality that originally made him successful.

SOLUTION   As his business grew, Paul and his design teams took deliberate steps away from starchy, formulaic fashion marketing. Together, they exchanged idea for idea, thrived on spontaneity, and diligently groomed the brand fabric.

RESULT   Starting with a quaint 12-foot by 12-foot shop, Paul Smith showed the fashion industry how modest growth and honest good taste are strong threads to a seamless brand.

PAUL SMITH designer and chairman [PAUL SMITH LTD]
ALAN ABOUD creative director [ABOUD SODANO]

JOE DUFFY Your brand's visual language over time has maintained an admirable level of consistency, purity, and honesty. Tell me how you managed to do that all this time?

PAUL SMITH We're still a privately owned business, owned by my wife and me. When you're not the slave of shareholders and people looking for more increase in business every year, you have more freedom to express yourself spontaneously.

DUFFY And spontaneity for you means honesty. That really comes across in your communications. The purity, the honesty, and being about not only your unique product, but also about your relationship with an audience that loves your product. That is rare in branding.

SMITH Unfortunately, the world is on such a fast track all the time, with everyone trying to keep up with everybody else. They did that, so we must do that. We've got to move fast on this. Oddly enough, we're quite quaint. It's the perfect world: We are in the clothes business and we like to increase our business every year, but that is never the driving force. The driving force is simply having a nice business that we enjoy.

DUFFY With a brand that is so personal and so much about you and your wife, how do you let someone in and inform them in a way that they can in effect create a voice for your brand?

SMITH In the beginning my wife and I were involved in the

design of everything, including the invitation cards — any form of graphics related to the company — and we had absolutely no money for advertising anywhere. That carried on for a long time. Most of the pictures we used I had taken while on holiday in Greece. We used a picture of a guy having a shave in a backstreet in Italy and things like that, so the invitation cards really were very personal. I kept thinking, well, there's this guy called Paul Smith. Nobody knows who the heck he is, so if I'm sending an invitation card to *Vogue* magazine or to *Elle* magazine, what are the chances that it'll end up in the bin? I thought if I could do an invite that was more like a postcard or something humorous, then people might at least stick it on their pin boards. That keeps my name on the wall for five minutes more than if it had gone in the bin. So it was very personal.

Then the business grew, and we were looking for additional help in graphics. Suddenly there were more than just invitation cards. There was a little catalog or brochure required for our business in Japan. Then I came across Alan Aboud and Sandro Sodano during their degree program at the St. Martin's School of Art. I employed Alan as a freelance graphics designer and hired Sandro for freelance photography work.

DUFFY Were you looking for a firm to help you out in that regard?

SMITH No, we weren't looking at all.

Paul Smith

DUFFY You just happened to go to their degree program?

SMITH I go to a lot of the college shows. I set up Paul Smith scholarships.

DUFFY When did you start sponsoring scholarships?

SMITH A long time ago, about 15 years ago in fact. My wife and I are very close to the Royal College of Art and to the Slade School at the Royal Academy of Arts.

DUFFY Alan, when did you start working with Paul Smith?

ALAN ABOUD Some 14 years ago. Paul was looking for a new designer to help them with their print needs. He, along with his head buyer, Patricia Keating, interviewed several others and myself just coming out of school. It's funny, I was probably the one person that was completely wrong for the job. I mean, if you looked at it on paper, based on my experience at the time, I wasn't really what he needed. He does that a lot. He has made many decisions over the years that seem to be wrong. But his instincts have proven to be so very right. That's part of his success.

He's good at a number of things. He's a shopkeeper. He's a designer. He's a businessman. His wife says, "It's like spinning plates in the circus." In the end, it's really his energy and positive attitude that drive the business and have made his brand successful.

PAUL SMITH

DUFFY Paul, as you pointed out, before you brought Alan on board you had a very personal business. You were making all the decisions. How did you adjust to having Alan do the work you were accustomed to doing?

SMITH I'm not a confrontational person; I'm quite a down-to-earth guy. I was losing out because I wasn't getting what I felt I wanted, so I had to learn to say what I liked about the work and what I didn't like. I'd ask Alan to try this or that as well. We'd discuss it. Talking it through a week in advance and agreeing on everything helped us both embrace the work.

DUFFY So it's a collaboration where the work gets better because you both contribute.

SMITH Correct. A properly balanced partnership of effort and result.

DUFFY Sounds like you developed a process. How has that changed things?

SMITH Because I'd never really trained in anything at all — I left school at 15 — I hadn't experienced organization and how to work with people or run a business. It was really shooting from the hip every time. Just learning.

DUFFY Inventing it on the fly, as you were.

SMITH Learning by doing it, and therefore, opening up the work to the world, both for the person doing the work and

MANUFACTURED AND DISTRIBUTED BY YOSHINAGA CORPORATION
INFORMATION: PAUL SMITH JAPAN 03-3486-1500

Paul Smith
BAG

MANUFACTURED AND DISTRIBUTED BY YOSHINAGA CORPORATION
INFORMATION: PAUL SMITH JAPAN 03-3486-1500

Paul Smith
BAG

for me so that in the end we were both very happy and very satisfied with the results.

DUFFY Do you use this approach in both your product design teams and your graphic design teams?

SMITH Yeah, I do it with everything. I do it in personal situations and in business situations.

DUFFY Do you bring in Alan and his group at the early stages when you're still thinking conceptually about the next line of clothing?

SMITH Yes. For instance, just in designing the clothes, I'm now working on next Spring. So, three weeks ago I had a meeting with my two main product designers, one for women and one for men. We lock ourselves in a hotel in the countryside in the north of England for two days, and I go armed with found samples — old books, photographs, words, poems, videos, CDs, anything — and talk about what they mean to me and how I see them influencing the next line. Then the designers go off and begin initial sketches. Very soon after that, I begin briefing Alan to get him involved in the thought process. That way, if he's looking through a bookshop and sees something he likes, he might buy that book. I also do that with the people who organize the fashion shows as well as the window dressers, so they begin to get the seed of the idea. I think that's how it works.

Eventually, you know that once all the people are involved,

FISH PRINT HAT £28, FISH PRINT DRESS £40/45, ORANGE JERSEY JACKET £40/45.

GILET £30/35, 'GLOW IN THE DARK' DINOSAUR T-SHIRT £22/28, TOP £40/45, REVERSE-PRINT DENIM JEANS £40/45.

ORANGE SPIDER ON THE BACK BABY T-SHIRT £28.

Paul Smith
WOMEN

you're not going to get 100 percent of what you have in your heart. You have to live with that. As soon as you involve other people, you have to appreciate that they have a talent and they have a point of view, too.

DUFFY How would you describe the Paul Smith brand?

ABOUD It's really about individuality. The brand is really a reflection of Paul himself. He's quite eclectic. He always sees new things and sees them in an inspired way. You should see his office. It's full of toys and music and books and images. There's stuff everywhere. Piles. In many ways, his office is like a visual interpretation of his mind—organized chaos. If you ask him where something is, he's quickly able to find it — in the pile behind the water cooler, under the table, to the left.

Over time, much as we don't like it, the brand has been labeled, "classic with a twist." But as I think about it, it's really the best way to describe it. Everything that's Paul Smith has a bit of humor in it, something a little unexpected. Maybe there is something almost surreal about it, but not too over the top.

DUFFY You talked about the process and how you are able to draw the voice of the brand out of the people that work with you. It must be doubly difficult to maintain the voice that you know so well and that other people can't possibly know to the degree that you do.

SMITH It's quite a unique business though. Again, I think we can be described as quaint or old-fashioned, because in fact, we are a relatively small business in the world of fashion. I'm completely involved in every aspect of the business and obviously that is a danger for the future of my business. So, I'm slowly tucking under me people like Alan and people like the assistant designers, so they get the spirit of Paul Smith, the certain individuality about it.

DUFFY **As you've added people to your team, has the voice of your brand changed or has the business changed?**

SMITH In certain periods of the last 25 to 30 years, there have been times when I might have felt a bit insecure for some reason — maybe in the heady early '90s, when a lot of the very big fashion brands were being created through the mass-marketing process. Very large sums of money were being thrown at brands with a very modern-man and modern-woman look. I felt a bit old-fashioned at the time because a lot of my look was quintessential English. Yes, there are certain times when I feel quite vulnerable and not quite so strong with my overall vision and voice. But then I get my breath back and move to the next stage.

For example, at the beginning of every season, I talk directly to the staff about the men's and women's collections. I talk to the sales staff and the shop staff. I'm in this building walking around all the time where we have 140 people, so I think there's more direct contact and more of a direct line to me than a lot of other companies.

KEEP WARM

Buy at the Paul Smith Winter Sale

Radiator connected to 2-in. Cast Pipe on the Single Pipe System.

DUFFY Your shop seems to be a good example of what your brand is all about — the fixturing, the product displays, the way the shops actually take on a personality. It's all truly consistent with the product and with your vision. How do you achieve that?

SMITH The first shop was in 1970, and it was 12 foot square. It was only open on Fridays and Saturdays, and it was just clothes I liked. I used to go on backpacking holidays with the kids to Greece, and I'd go into a stationery shop and find some old notebooks and pen knives that a farmer might use, or some funny rugs made from rags, and I'd bring them back and put them in my shop to make it look a little different than somebody else's shop. Without realizing it, I was starting the quirkiness and the lateral thinking and the unusual approach to Paul Smith.

The shops have their own quirkiness because we approach each without a formula. We say, "Okay, this shop is in Milan, how should it look?" So the Milan shop has dusty pink walls and a mosaic floor like you might find in a church.

I loathe the corporate rollout, and I just loathe the idea of everything being the same. Paul Smith is about individuality. Paul Smith is about your wearing the clothes rather than the clothes wearing you. I think for a lot of brands the clothes wear you. Those kinds of brands say, "I am part of a club, or I am wealthy, or I am fashionable." I hope my clothes say, "I am me."

That's why we sell to bankers and other very serious businessmen, and we sell to rock bands, to Travis, Coldplay, Mick Jagger, David Bowie, Madonna, and Julia Roberts. We sell to a massive range of people because they are allowed to wear the clothes in their own way.

DUFFY Is there any formula at all that you bring into a shop that you open?

SMITH For factual things like the number of cash registers, changing rooms, hanging garments, flat garments, yes, but nothing else. I've got one guy who works full-time for me finding furniture and one guy who shops for me full-time. Nice job. Antique books, records, vinyls or CDs, objects. They go to places like Hungary, Milan, Verona, and Mount Pelier, just to visit antique fairs. That keeps the shops really individual and fresh. I suppose the formula is that there is no formula.

DUFFY In your mind, how has the Paul Smith brand evolved over time?

ABOUD One of the biggest influences on the brand has been its success in Japan. Not just because it's such a fabulous market, with a great respect and appreciation for design, but because it's made us realize that this brand needs to speak universally. It can't be language-specific. That's probably one of the reasons why so much of the advertising has so little copy in it.

And it goes back to the idea of individuality as well. There's so much fashion in Japan — and many other markets, for that matter — but so much of it is the same. I mean, you go to a city and you see Gucci and Prada and Chanel. And you see it in many places. It feels very uninspired.

Paul Smith has a certain amount of consistency to the brand. It has to. When there's a suit that works, you stick with the cut, but you evolve the fabric or the color of the lining. And the stores that sell it need to feel like Paul Smith, but they also need to fit into the environment. So when you think about it that way, it's about consistency, not replication. And that's what allows for individuality all the time as well. It's because of this — and Paul's curiosity and vision — that things like Westbourne House come to life and can change fashion and shopping and even neighborhoods.

DUFFY   Tell me more about Westbourne House.

ABOUD   Well, you see, Paul had this idea that he wanted to buy a house and make it into a store. This was another case where, for so many reasons, it seemed like the wrong decision. The finances didn't support it. The location didn't seem to make sense, as at the time, Notting Hill was all family, residential. The architect that he chose to partner with really didn't have any experience doing something like this either. But Paul had this idea and the energy and will to make it succeed. And he did. Now the whole of Notting Hill is just filled with young, fashion-minded girls shopping on Saturday mornings.

I have this joke with Paul, that he has a knack for ruining things, like my neighborhood, because I live in Notting Hill. He did the same with Covent Garden. That's where his main office is. It used to be a fruit-and-vegetable market. Now it's teeming with businesses all over.

DUFFY What is your favorite campaign or program from over the years? Do any stand out in your mind?

SMITH The work we did with David Bailey. It was black-and-white portraits of real people. It was very nice.

ABOUD I think that work was really great. Bailey was fantastic to work with, and I take a bit of pride in being able to get him to do portraiture for the Paul Smith project. He's still doing more in that area today. This relationship has really given me a chance to work with a number of fabulous photographers over the years. That's been something I've really enjoyed.

And the Gary Fisher bike. I loved that. It wasn't a deal driven by business motivations. Paul is just into biking. And Gary Fisher is a great guy. Very down-to-earth and real. They're both free spirits. That's what was so great about the project. It was just the three of us, working together, doing something creative because we were into it, and we really enjoyed working with each other.

And I guess I'm really proud of the book, *You Can Find Inspiration in Anything.* That there was such a great opportunity to write about Paul Smith — the man, not the brand — and that they asked me to be a part of it. And, that my team was able to rise to the occasion to wrestle this huge project to the ground and do such a great job.

DUFFY Do you worry about communicating the brand in such a way that it will feel as though it's not exclusive to the audience that has been with you for so many years?

SMITH To be honest, the whole point of choosing a theme or a type of communication has always been quite a concern to me. If it were left to me personally, I'd probably do something very, very wacky, or very odd, or personal, which wouldn't do the job at all. Still, we used to take a stand at a trade fair in Paris called Sehm, but we would break all the rules. One time we took a very expensive stand with an iron and an ironing board. Then, on the wall we put a Post-it note, where you could make an appointment to come see the collection.

FOREWARD

↓

My two-year journey studying the best of the best, and talking to the people behind the scenes in making them happen, leaves me both humbled and inspired. Humbled by the unbridled brilliance that is a result of their efforts. Inspired by what is possible when the highest levels of collaboration and creativity are aligned to tackle a challenge and create a big idea. Lessons learned here are immutable truths – ones which we can carry forward forever – no matter how the world around us changes, no matter what discipline is our specialty, no matter what challenge confronts us.

So what are the insights learned from this undeniably brilliant work? What advice can we take from the people on the front lines responsible for creating it? What can we learn from the moments of creative inspiration that have led to resoundingly consistent business results?

In a word – **respect.** Remember these principles of respect, and you can also create the all-too-rare chemistry that allows great work to be conceived, to be nurtured, and to blossom into something breathtakingly original.

Respect for the brand. Its history. Its equities. Its icons. What does the brand truly mean to people? What is its essence and *raison d'etre*? Always pushing the brand to reinvent itself and evolve. But never forgetting that the brand is a sum of all it has done in the past. All these sensational cases showed a deep understanding of the past, present and future of the brand.

Respect for the customer. Who are these people? What are their loves, fears, thoughts and dreams? What is important in their lives? What do they expect from the brand and what do they want the brand to be? The customer owes you little. You owe them everything. All these examples demonstrated enormous respect for the intelligence, time and values of the customer.

Respect for the value of collaboration. Can this client – creative partnership be based on mutual respect and create the kinetic energy that happens when a client and creative partner are truly on the same page? The great work and great results profiled happened because there wasn't an adversarial relationship between client and communication partner. The opposite is true. They fed each other, encouraged each other, debated long and hard and believed passionately in the power of a big idea to transform a business.

They exhibited collaboration, open-mindedness, courage and passion in everything they did. And in the end, they had fun doing it.

Finally, respect for the power of the craft. In every instance, these powerfully effective efforts brought together people of different skill sets, orientations and disciplines to seize the day and do something magical. In every instance, these people rose above their respective roles, titles or specialties and worked collaboratively on behalf of a big idea for the brand. They worked through the natural tensions that result when you form a cross-disciplinary team of many different perspectives. And they found a way to harness the collective talent and energy that resulted from those tensions to find new and different ways of thinking about the brand. In all cases, the result was a unique, brand-perfect way to go to market. Hearing the war stories and the recollections, you feel a deep and abiding respect for the collection of crafts that came together to create something magical.

Lessons learned from the frontlines of greatness – where great work and great results have come from seamless marketing communications. Making each one truly a Brand Apart.

JOE DUFFY

PHOTOS

ALAN ABOUD co-founder [ABOUD SODANO]

Alan Aboud is co-founder of Aboud Sodano, the creative team behind fashion designer Paul Smith's advertising campaigns as well as his brand's identity. Founded with Sandro Sodano in 1989, the studio specializes in design, photography and advertising. The two have collaborated on Web sites, product packaging, magazines and books, among their many projects. In 2002 Aboud began a creative alliance between Aboud Sodano and the New York agency, YARD. While each agency retains their existing clients separately, Aboud and YARD Creative Director, Stephen Niedzweicki collaborate together on international accounts and projects. Aboud studied design at London's St. Martin's School of Art, where he met Sodano. The duo has won many awards, including the New York Art Director's Club Silver Cube award, the Art Director's Club in Europe's Gold Award and two D+AD Awards. (Photo by Sandro Sodano)

DANA ARNETT principal [VSA PARTNERS]

Dana Arnett is a founding Principal of VSA Partners, headquartered in Chicago. Arnett, along with his four partners, leads a group of 70 associates in the creation of design programs, film projects, interactive initiatives and brand marketing solutions for a diverse roster of clients, including Harley-Davidson, IBM, General Electric, Coca-Cola, Cingular Wireless, Chronicle Books, and Time Warner. Over the course of his 21 years in the field, Dana and the firm have been globally recognized by over 60 competitions and designations including Communication Arts, AIGA, Graphis, The Type Directors Club, the American and British Art Directors Clubs, ID, The LA Film Festival, the AR100 and the American Marketing Association. Arnett was a 1999 inductee into the Alliance Graphic International, and holds the honor of being named to the I.D. 40 — who has cited him as one of the 40 most important people shaping design internationally. Arnett is also a member of the AIGA National Board of Directors, where he is involved in leadership and policy making that shapes the design industry.

BRUCE BILDSTEN former creative director [FALLON]

Bruce Bildsten was formerly Creative Director of Fallon's Minneapolis headquarters, with responsibility for the entire creative staff and direct responsibility for the BMW and PBS accounts. His work has won top honors at the most prestigious advertising creative competitions throughout his career. In 2001, Bruce won an Emmy Award for outstanding television commercial as both writer and creative director. He subsequently led the creative teams that won the Emmy in 2003 and 2004 as well. In March 2003, Bruce led the team that created the highly acclaimed BMW Films and was named one of the "Fast 50" by *Fast Company* magazine, a collection of the world's 50 "champions of innovation" in business and technology. Married, and a dedicated father of two, Bruce is an avid cyclist, skier and kayaker. He was a 1981 Phi Beta Kappa graduate of the University of Minnesota School of Journalism.

ALEX BOGUSKY creative director [CRISPIN PORTER+BOGUSKY]

Alex Bogusky started at what was then called Crispin and Porter Advertising in 1987 as an art director. He became Creative Director of the agency five years later and was named a partner in 1997. Under his direction, the agency has become arguably one of the world's most awarded. Alex has been profiled in *Luerzer's Archive*, *Communication Arts*, *Graphis*, *Adweek* and *Creativity*. His work has been featured in *The New York Times*, *The Wall Street Journal*, *USA Today*, *Newsweek*, *TIME*, *Adweek*, *Brandweek*, *Advertising Age* and *Creativity* as well as on national television and radio. In 2002, Alex was inducted into the American Advertising Federation's Hall of Achievement.

BRIAN COLLINS executive creative director
[OGILVY & MATHER WORLDWIDE / BRAND INTEGRATION GROUP]

Brian Collins is Executive Creative Director at Ogilvy & Mather Worldwide, where he leads the Brand Integration Group, the agency's design and brand experience division. BIG works with some of the world's most prominent brands, including American Express, IBM, The Miller Brewing Company, Dove, Jaguar, Coca-Cola, Hershey Foods, and Kodak. With offices in New York and Los Angeles, the team's recent work includes the design of the fifteen-story tall Hershey chocolate factory in Times Square and, for Dove, the traveling photography exhibit "Beyond Compare" highlighting the work of the world's leading women photographers. Brian's team also designed the *New York Times* bestseller, *Brotherhood*, a pictorial review of the lives of the city's firefighters in the aftermath of 9/11. Brian's team was also awarded New York City's identity design program for the 2012 Olympics bid. The team's work has won every major creative award, has been exhibited in the Cooper Hewitt National Museum of Design, and has been featured on CBS, NBC, *USA Today* and the *New York Times*. Brian speaks internationally on branding and design and teaches at the School of Visual Arts.

LEE ANN DALY executive vice president, marketing [ESPN]

Lee Ann Daly has served as Executive Vice President of Marketing at ESPN since April 2004. She is responsible for the development, direction and implementation of all branding, creative services and marketing for ESPN's growing media businesses. She is also responsible for the company's growing media businesses. She is also responsible for the company's synergy efforts including brand management of ESPN-branded business activities supported by The Walt Disney Company, including the ESPN Zones. Daly and her team are responsible for the development of over 50 marketing campaigns annually including the award-winning "This is SportsCenter" and most recently, "Without Sports," which celebrates the role of sports in society. In 2004, she also oversaw the development of ESPN's ongoing "The Season of the Fan" campaign as part of ESPN's 25th Anniversary celebration. Daly also played an important role in the launch and development of ESPN's Original Entertainment division. Daly has served as a member of ESPN's executive committee since 2001.

KEVIN FLATT creative director, interactive [FALLON]

As a part of Fallon since 1995, Kevin Flatt has been creating work for clients such as Amazon.com, Archipelago, BMW of North America, The Bahamas Ministry of Tourism, EDS, United Airlines, Miller Brewing Company, International Trucks, Lee Jeans, RJ Reynolds, McDonald's, Microsoft and Timberland. His work has received recognition from many respected industry competitions and publications, including *Communication Arts, Graphis, TIME, Adweek*, the Type Directors Club, The Art Directors Club, Clio, the One Show Best of Show, Cannes Grand Prix and first-ever Titanium Cyber Lion for BMW Films. Kevin is actively involved in the community, speaking at industry conferences and judging notable industry competitions, including the One Show and Cannes.

VANESSA HARMATZ panrtner/management supervisor [OGILVY & MATHER]

Vanessa Harmatz is Partner and Management Supervisor at Ogilvy & Mather in New York. She has been with Ogilvy for over four years, working exclusively on the ONDCP campaign and the New York Public Library. Vanessa currently oversees the general market youth and parent audiences and has been an integral part of some of the campaign's greatest successes, including the youth brand launch, the drugs and terror launch, and formulation and implementation of the drug diary study which led to innovative and groundbreaking creative and media changes. Vanessa also developed advertising for the New York Public Library, on both adult literacy and youth summer reading efforts. Prior to coming to Ogilvy, Vanessa spent four years at Messner Euro RSCG leading unbranded telecom work for MCI targeting teens and young adults. Vanessa attended the University of Delaware, studied Spanish in Costa Rica for a semester and was the recipient of the Order of the Owl Award for academic excellence.

JOHN C. JAY *partner/executive creative director*
[WIEDEN + KENNEDY]

John C. Jay is a Partner and Executive Creative Director for Wieden + Kennedy. Previously, he served for 5 years as Executive Creative Director for the Tokyo office. In 2003, Jay launched the agency's independent DVD music label, W+K TokyoLab and in 2004, he opened the W+K office in Shanghai. He has been named as one of "40 Most Influential" in design by *I.D. magazine* in the U.S., once noted as one of "80 Most Influential" by *American Photographer* magazine and his book, *Soul of the Game* was awarded in 1997 as one of the "14 Most Beautiful Books in the World" by the Copenhagan Museum. His work has appeared as a part of exhibitions in museums and galleries in New York, Chicago, Portland, Boston, Paris, London, St. Petersburg and Frankfurt.

DAVID LUBARS *chairman and chief creative officer*
[BBDO NORTH AMERICA]

David Lubars is Chairman and Chief Creative Officer for BBDO North America. Previously, he was president of Fallon Worldwide and Executive Creative Director of Fallon North America. Since joining Fallon as Creative Director in 1998, David helped win the Citibank, Nestle/Purina, PBS, Dyson, Navistar International, and EDS accounts, and personally added Starbucks and Amazon to the agency roster. He also helps run the agency's pro-bono work for Camp Heartland, a camp for children affected by HIV and AIDS. David has won every major creative award in the world including Grand Prix Cannes, Grand Clio, Grand Andy, One Show Best of Show, Best of Show Radio Mercury, Gold Effie, British D&AD, Communications Arts and the Emmy two times for Best TV Commercial in America. His work has been written about in the *New York Times*, *The Wall Street Journal*, *USA Today* and *TIME* magazine, and has appeared on the cover of *Archive* magazine twice. In 2003, his BMW work was made part of MoMA's permanent collection in New York City and he won the first-ever awarded Titanium Lion at Cannes. David lives in New York City with his wife, Cindy, and two sons, Michael and Alex.

ANNE MACDONALD *managing director of global marketing*
[CITIGROUP]

Anne MacDonald is the Managing Director of Global Marketing for the consumer businesses at Citigroup, which she joined in October 1997. Prior to joining Citibank, she spent five years with PepsiCo, where she was in charge of brand management and communication for the Pizza Hut division. Anne joined PepsiCo following thirteen years with the privately held advertising agency, N.W. Ayer. While there, she held senior roles across client businesses in the consumer package goods, telecommunications, financial services, luxury goods, and business-to-business categories, among others. During her tenure at N.W. Ayer, Anne was elected to the Board of Directors. Prior to N.W. Ayer, Anne worked in the international division of Grey Advertising in New York. Anne did her undergraduate studies at Boston College and received her Master's in Business from Bath University in England.

KERRI MARTIN director of brand innovation
[VOLKSWAGEN OF AMERICA]

Kerri Martin joined the BMW Group in 1997 as the Brand and Events Marketing Manager for BMW Motorcycles. She was bit by the automotive bug in August 2000 when she was promoted to MINI USA's 'Guardian of Brand Soul', a.k.a. Director of Marketing, which charged her with the responsibility of re-launching the MINI brand in the United States. Her experience with exhilarating, iconic and distinctive motor vehicles was forged in part during her previous tenure in the marketing department at the Harley-Davidson Motor Company. At Harley she was responsible for the marketing of Harley's extensive private label line of MotorClothes and accessories. Kerri is currently at Volkswagen where she is the head of marketing development. Kerri graduated with honors from the University of Wisconsin-Madison in 1992 and was named as one of *Advertising Age's* "Women to Watch" in 2004.

JAMES L. MCDOWELL vice president of MINI division
[MINI USA]

James L. McDowell is Vice President of MINI and was formerly Vice President of Marketing for BMW of North America. At the beginning of 1993, Mr. McDowell joined BMW AG's planning group in Munich, Germany. Previously, he served as Director of Marketing at Porsche AG in Stuttgart, Germany. Prior to that he held managerial positions for OCLI from 1984 to 1985 and with GTE from 1981 to 1984. He was named "Marketer of the Year" in 2003 by *Automotive News*, and he was twice named "Marketer of the Year" by *Brandweek* magazine. The Advertising Club named him the "2003 Silver Medal Advertising Man of the Year." James earned a bachelor's degree in behavioral psychology from Colorado College and a master's degree in public policy analysis and administration from Harvard University.

KEVIN RODDY executive creative director [BBH]

Prior to his current position as Executive Creative Director at BBH, Kevin Roddy worked at Euro RSCG, Fallon and Cliff Freeman writing for clients ranging from Little Caesars to Volvo, Timberland to *TIME* magazine, FOX Sports, Staples, Starbucks and others. As a writer, Kevin has been responsible for some of the most awarded campaigns in recent years, winning every major award around the globe several times over including the One Show, D&AD and Cannes. Most notably, Kevin is the only person to ever win the One Show's "Best of Show" twice.

STEVE SANDSTROM partner/creative director [SANDSTROM DESIGN]

Steve Sandstrom is Creative Director and Partner of Sandstrom Design in Portland, Oregon. Clients have included Tazo, Levi Strauss & Co., Converse, ESPN, Miller Brewing, Nike, Seagram's, Steppenwolf Theatre, adidas International, Nissan, Coca-Cola, Virgin, Microsoft and Sony Pictures. Prior to founding Sandstrom Design in November 1988, he was a senior art director at Nike, primarily responsible for brand image and collateral materials for the apparel division.

PAULA SCHER principal [PENTAGRAM]

Paula Scher has been a principal of Pentagram since 1991. Scher has developed identity and branding systems, promotional materials, environmental graphics, packaging and publication designs for a broad range of clients that includes, among others, the *New York Times Magazine*, Citibank, Bloomberg, the Asia Society, Jazz at Lincoln Center, Perry Ellis, the Detroit Symphony Orchestra, the New Jersey Performing Arts Center, the New 42nd Street, and "The Daily Show with Jon Stewart." Her work is represented in the permanent collections of the Museum of Modern Art and the Cooper-Hewitt National Design Museum, New York; the Library of Congress, Washington, D.C.; the Museum für Gestaltung Zürich; the Denver Art Museum; and the Bibliothèque nationale de France and the Centre Georges Pompidou, Paris. Scher's teaching career includes over two decades at the School of Visual Arts, along with positions at the Cooper Union, Yale University and the Tyler School of Art. She has authored numerous articles on design-related subjects for the *AIGA Journal of Graphic Design, Print, Graphis*, and other publications, and in 2002 Princeton Architectural Press published her career monograph, *Make It Bigger*. (Photo by Jens Umbach)

KIM SCHOEN freelance art director

Kim Schoen is a freelance art director currently pursuing her Masters in Fine Arts in photography at the California Institute for the Arts. In 2003, she freelanced as a Group Creative Director at BBH New York. Prior to that, she was an Associate Creative Director at Wieden + Kennedy/New York, where she worked on campaigns for ESPN, Nike, Avon and the School of Visual Arts. Her campaigns for Nike, ESPN, and Levi's have garnered awards in *Communication Arts* magazine, D&AD, the One Show; won Gold at Cannes, have been featured in *i-D* magazine, *ZOO, The Creative Review, Shoot, Boards,* and *Photo District News*. She has worked abroad at W+K Amsterdam, on clients such as Hypovereinsbank, Siemens, and Nike. She began her career at Foote Cone & Belding in San Francisco where she art directed national television and print campaigns for Levi's Jeans and Dockers K-1 Khakis. She has guest art-directed *SOMA* magazine, served as an adjunct professor at The School of Visual Arts, and has worked for *i-D* magazine in London.

PAUL SMITH designer/chairman [PAUL SMITH]

Paul Smith, Designer and Chairman, managed his first boutique in Nottingham and opened his own tiny shop in 1970. By 1976, Paul showed his first menswear collection in Paris under the Paul Smith label. Within 20 years of his introduction to fashion, Paul Smith had established himself as the pre-eminent British designer. Paul Smith is global — the collection is wholesaled to 35 countries and has 14 shops in England. Paul Smith shops are found in London, Nottingham, England. Paul Smith shops are found in London, Nottingham, Paris, Milan, New York, Hong Kong, Singapore, Taiwan, the Philippines, Korea, Kuwait, U.A.E. — and over 200 throughout Japan. Paul remains fully involved in the Japanese business, designing the clothes, choosing the fabrics, approving the shop locations and overseeing every development within the company. Paul Smith also has impressive and diverse showrooms in London, Paris, Milan, New York, and Tokyo. (Photo by Mischa Richter)

STEVE SMITH founder [TAZO]

Steve Smith has spent more than 30 years immersed in the subtleties of tea. Smith was one of the founders of Stash Tea Company in 1972. Inspired by the success of Stash, in 1994 Smith set out to upgrade the tea experience by creating a super-premium tea brand, Tazo. Tazo was named "Best Product Line" by the Specialty Coffee Association of America in 1995 and 1996. Today, Smith is recognized internationally as one of the industry's leading tea entrepreneurs.

VINCENT VANDERPOOL-WALLACE director general
[MINISTRY OF TOURISM/BAHAMAS]

Vincent Vanderpool-Wallace was appointed to the position of Director General of Tourism for The Bahamas in January 1993. Born in Nassau, Mr. Vanderpool-Wallace attended the Government High School, where he won the Princeps Prize for scholarship and later graduated with a Bachelor's Degree cum laude from Harvard University in May 1975. He received his MBA from the University of Miami in 1981. Mr. Vanderpool-Wallace began his full-time employment at the Ministry of Education and Culture and later joined the Ministry of Tourism. Mr. Vanderpool-Wallace was named Person of The Year for the Caribbean by *Travel Agent* magazine in 1998 and served for many years as Chairman of The Marketing Committee of the Caribbean Tourism Organization (CTO). In January 2001, he received the Albert E Koehl Award for Lifetime Achievement in Advertising by Hospitality Sales & Marketing Association International (HSMAI). In May 2001, he received the Atlas Award for Lifetime Achievement from the Association of Travel Marketing Executives International.

TOM WATSON marketing director [HARLEY DAVIDSON]

Tom Watson is Marketing Director at Harley-Davidson Motor Company with responsibilities over Harley-Davidson & Buell motorcycles, and Harley-Davidson MotorClothes apparel. In the ten years that he has been with Harley-Davidson, he has been involved in the planning and execution of Harley's 95th & 100th Anniversary celebration events, all national and dealer advertising, as well as overall brand issues. Prior to joining Harley-Davidson, Tom Watson worked for Leo Burnett Advertising in Chicago on diverse accounts including Kraft, RCA Consumer Electronics and Keebler.

DAN WIEDEN president [WIEDEN + KENNEDY]

Dan Wieden began his career in public relations and then became a copywriter at a small Portland agency working on the Nike account with his partner David Kennedy. Dan and David then started their own agency with one small client and three other employees. Over two decades later, the agency now has offices in New York, London, Amsterdam, Tokyo and Shanghai. Wieden + Kennedy has won many awards over the years including the One Show awards and Dan Wieden has been celebrated as one of the most influential people in advertising.

AMY WIRTANEN director of bakery & food strategy [STARBUCKS]

Amy Wirtanen has been with the Starbucks Coffee Company since 2000 and, in her current role, is the Director of Bakery & Food Strategy for the North American Retail Food Category. Amy began her career at Starbucks working as Marketing Manager and then Director, Marketing Innovation with the North American Coffee Partnership, a joint venture between Starbucks Coffee Company and Pepsi Cola North America. Prior to Starbucks, Amy spent four years in international and domestic marketing roles at Ernest & Julio Gallo Winery in Modesto, California. During her tenure there she managed a portfolio of brands in key European countries, held the role of marketing manager for the Turning Leaf Coastal Reserve/ Turning Leaf brands, and led new product development initiatives. Amy holds a Master of Business Administration from the Darden Graduate School of Business Administration at the University of Virginia and a Bachelor of Arts from the University of Michigan.

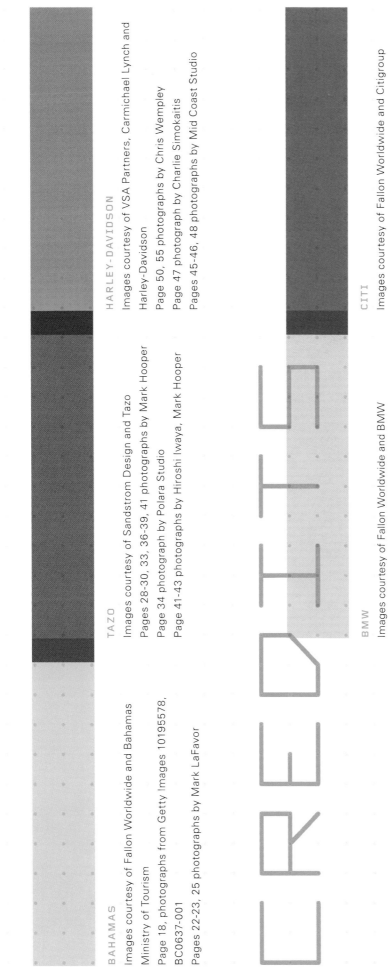

CREDITS

BAHAMAS

Images courtesy of Fallon Worldwide and Bahamas Ministry of Tourism

Page 18, photographs from Getty Images 10195578, BC0637-001

Pages 22-23, 25 photographs by Mark LaFavor

TAZO

Images courtesy of Sandstrom Design and Tazo

Pages 28-30, 33, 36-39, 41 photographs by Mark Hooper

Page 34 photograph by Polara Studio

Page 41-43 photographs by Hiroshi Iwaya, Mark Hooper

HARLEY-DAVIDSON

Images courtesy of VSA Partners, Carmichael Lynch and Harley-Davidson

Page 50, 55 photographs by Chris Wempley

Page 47 photograph by Charlie Simokaitis

Pages 45-46, 48 photographs by Mid Coast Studio

BMW

Images courtesy of Fallon Worldwide and BMW North America

Page 62 photographs by Michael Crouser

Pages 66-67, 70-71 photographs by Mark LaFavor

CITI

Images courtesy of Fallon Worldwide and Citigroup

Pages 84-85 photographs by Chris Buck

Page 79 image courtesy of Pentagram Design

NIKE

Images courtesy of Wieden + Kennedy and Nike

Pages 92-94, 98-101 images courtesy of Wieden + Kennedy/Tokyo and Nike

Pages 87, 90, 91 photographs by Michael Jones

Page 94 photograph by Kazuyasu Hagane

MINI

Images courtesy of Crispin Porter + Bogusky and MINI USA

Pages 106-110, 112-113, 116-117 photographs by Daniel Hartz

Page 104-105 photographs by Mark Laita and Daniel Hartz

Page 111 photograph by Tim Damon and Daniel Hartz

Page 114 illustrations by Timmy Kucynda

WHAT'S YOUR ANTI DRUG?

Images courtesy of Brand Integration Group/Ogilvy & Mather and The White House Office of National Drug Control Policy

Photo illustrations by Dan Hallman, Kevin Lyons and Patric Bolecek

STARBUCKS

Images courtesy of Fallon Worldwide and Starbucks

WINTER X-GAMES

Illustrations courtesy of Geoff McFetridge, Wieden+Kennedy and ESPN

PAUL SMITH

Images courtesy of Aboud-Sodano and Paul Smith

Pages 158-163 photographs by Sandro Sodano

Pages 164-165 photographs by David Bailey

INDEX

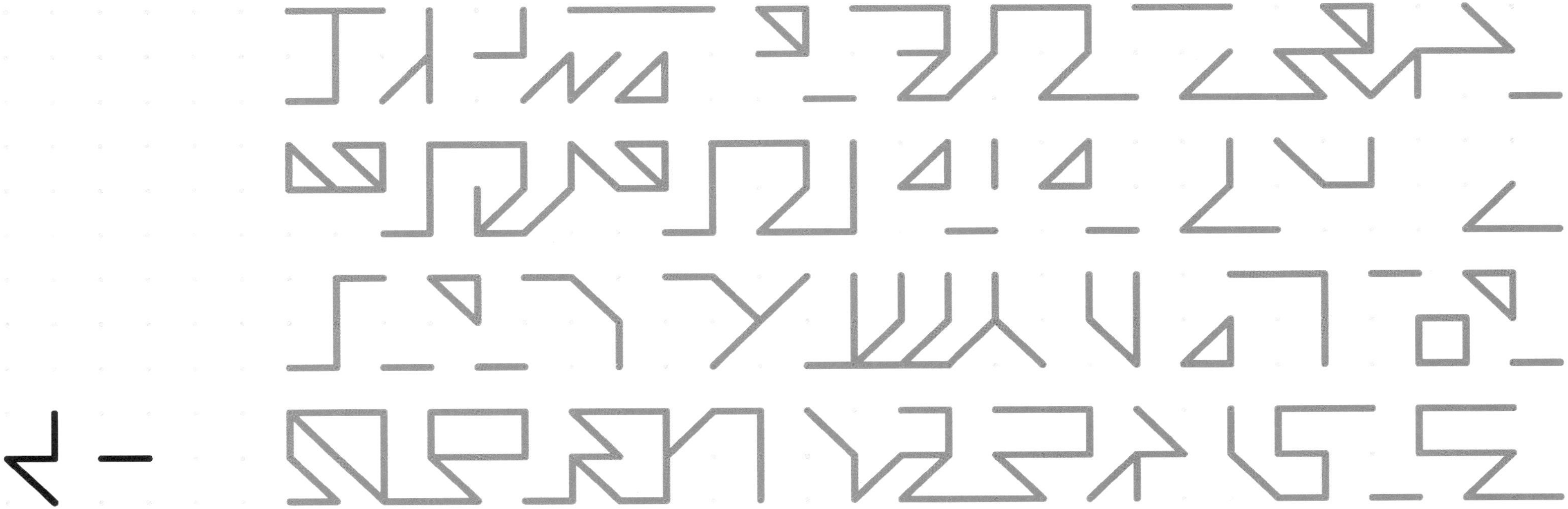

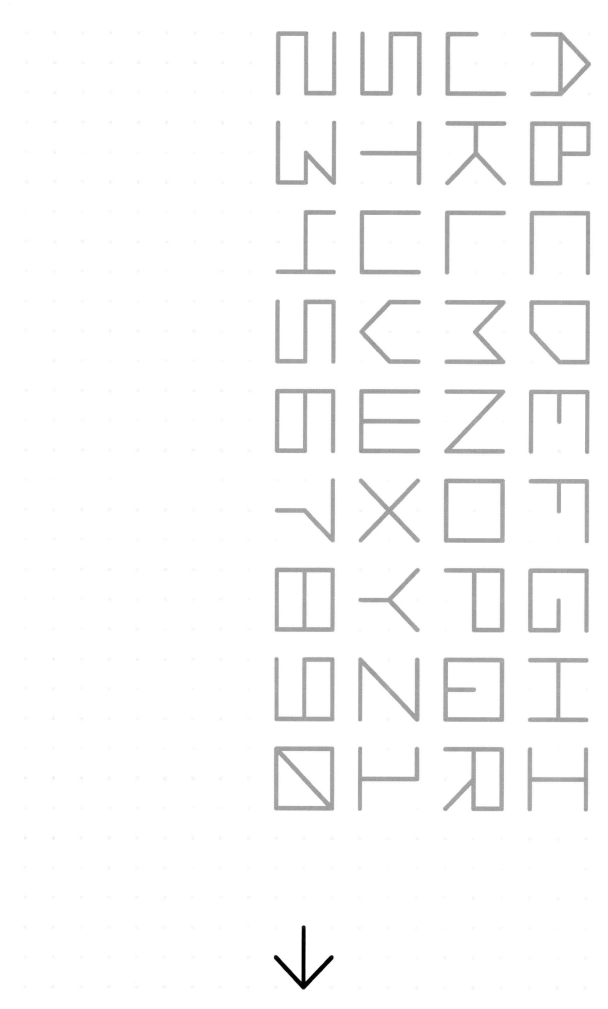